Beyond Mindfulness:
Living Life
through
Everyday Zen

Talks & Writings

Ken Jones

Alba Publishing

Published by Alba Publishing
P O Box 266, Uxbridge
UB9 5NX, United Kingdom
www.albapublishing.com

A catalogue record for this book is available from the British Library

ISBN: 978-1-910185-15-5

Edited, designed and typeset by Kim Richardson
Cover images: © 2015 Kim Richardson;
Printed by Bookpress.eu

10 9 8 7 6 5 4 3 2 1

Contents

Foreword

I first met Ken Jones at the beginning of this Millennium. He and I led a retreat together at Maenllwyd in mid-Wales, standing in for Chan Master John Crook. At the time Ken was thinking about new approaches to teaching the Dharma, making the practice of Zen relevant and useful to the everyday life of Westerners. We became good friends.

This book is the result of Ken's lifelong research and work with retreat participants to widen the traditional approach of sitting meditation. Ken encourages moving away from long periods of silent sitting towards engagement and relationship. He uses workshop-style exercises alongside meditation and draws on his understanding of the writing of Zen Master Dogen. Ken teaches how practice on the cushion can help when facing the issues and problems of daily life – living in families, dealing with the boss or managing close relationships. How can you use the difficulties and discomfitures of everyday life to "turn straw into gold"? The last chapter of the book shows how Ken's interest in Zen prose and poetry can express this work creatively.

Embrace the approach put forward in these essays and life will never be boring. The door will open to an exploration of being in the world and a dynamic acceptance of how it is to be you, fully engaged with life and following the Great Way.

Hilary Richards,
Retreat Leader for the Western Chan Fellowship

Introduction: How to Use this Book

This book is a package of talks and writings given and made over a considerable period rather than a beginning-to-end read. This format inevitably implies a certain amount of repetition, for which I ask the reader's forgiveness. I believe that different approaches to the theme signalled by the title will suit different readers. The straightforward approach would be to start with "How To Do Everyday Buddhism". This is a kind of do-it-yourself introduction which, in my experience teaching retreats, works equally well for people of other inner path spiritualities than Buddhism. The eight talks which follow were taken variously from my retreats. Since each, like that on relationships for example, is freestanding they offer a choiceful rather than a strictly sequential read. *Suchness and This vs. That,* which comes next, offers a deeper understanding founded on the teaching of Eihei Dogen, one of the greatest of Buddhism's philosopher-monks. It is also something of a beginner's guide to Dogen, whose writings can be quite difficult.

The piece on ageing was originally published as a pamphlet by the Buddhist Hospice Trust, and soon went out of print. My own subsequent experience of deeper ageing and terminal illness has confirmed to me that if you follow the instructions on the bottle, they do work. Life can certainly get particularly interesting after eighty, or even earlier.

Finally, for something novel, you may like to dive into the haiku prose writings at the end of this book. Nine of these offer experiences of Zen retreats over the years, including solitary ones and interviews. Another ten trace out my experience of a long drawn out terminal cancer. All are redolent of Zen Buddhism, and offer another way of sensing how it feels.

Ken Jones

How to Do Everyday Buddhism

This is an enlarged and updated version of an earlier text written for my website www.kenjoneszen.com. It has been prompted by new approaches and clarifications arising from retreats I have taught since then. The original text was intended as a kind of do-it-yourself manual both for would-be participants on my retreats (four or five day events) and for other interested readers. It also provides a foundation and introduction for other essays and papers on my website. These retreats have become something of a new and multi-faceted approach to the teaching of Buddhist practice, beyond their central concern with "Everyday Buddhism" and as spelt out in more detail on my website as *New Departures in Dharma Teaching and Practice*. With the advance of my prostate cancer I am no longer able to continue with my annual retreat programme at the half dozen or so hospitable centres available to me. So this seemed an opportunity to explain where I had got to, and to leave behind some kind of record.

Buddhist retreats traditionally consist of a talk by the teacher explaining some concept or practice, perhaps with anecdotal illustrations, and concluding with a question and answer session. The whole will commonly be reinforced by meditation sessions and perhaps one-to-one interviews. However, I believe that these *ideas* need to be more grounded in each student's life experience if they are to become an embodied and effective practice.

As a first step I invite each student to reflect — on and off the cushion — how the idea (for example "suchness") is, or might be, emotionally experienced in their lives, and particularly in the more discomfiting and grievous episodes. Later in the day they are invited to share their experience in groups of four or five, the discussion being regulated by a "speaking stone". They also work in pairs in which each takes it in turn always to ask the same question of the other and nothing more. "Tell me, so-and-so, how does it *feel*"? The feeling refers to whatever of life's discomfitures the student is currently deepening in her emotional awareness. Or it may be the more general question "how does it feel to be *you?*" This exercise can sometimes produce striking openings, though much depends on the skill and sensitivity of the questioner. The whole process is reinforced by intensive personal interviews, followed by further individual practice on or off the cushion. It takes place against a background of energetic group physical exercises characterised by awareness of the other and, incidentally, a lot of *fun* and tumbling about. From the first hours of the retreat I aim to build up a strong sense of fellowship and mutual confidence as an important emotional lubricant.

In the foregoing I have been inspired by the influential Zen teacher Norman Fischer:-

> These days, as I continue to teach Zen outside the traditional context of monastic life, I am trying to see what will work to bring ordinary people in the ordinary world to the sort of deeper, fuller living that Zen promises. I have found that it is of crucial importance for people to be able to express themselves fully... In recent years it has become clear to me that students need to do more than absorb teaching and ask clarifying questions. They need to speak to their hearts... Expression is healing. It opens us, propelling us forth into our lives. It's not so much a matter of ideas or even of feelings, for expression is more than a cognitive or emotional act. Yet somehow the simple act of speaking truly, out loud and to others, inspires us finally to point our prow out to sea as we set forth onward for the journey. (*Sailing Homes*, Free Press, 2008, p43).

This kind of teaching is absent from the teaching most post-modern Western students receive and I believe has seriously limited the effectiveness of much Buddhist teaching in the West. It is unlikely to work for most students with an Asian background and education who inhabit a rather different culture of personal relationship. In the West the adhesion to Asian cultural norms has cast a long shadow over what we teachers are trying to achieve.

This paper is a "manual" in that I have included at each stage "do-it-yourself" exercises to enable readers working on their own to make some trial of the methods I describe and to go more deeply and personally into what they have been reading.

"Everyday Buddhism" is not a new kind of Buddhism, but is hospitable to most Buddhist traditions and, indeed, to other inner path spiritualities. The Zen slant in these pages is no more than a reflection of my own practice, which has been particularly inspired by the thirteenth century master Eihei Dogen.

The self as the focus of study and meditation is central to everyday Buddhism in virtually all Buddhist traditions. To become familiar with one's unique emotional furniture and to trace the trajectory of one's lifelong but futile struggle to sustain a secure and enduring sense of self is the major diagnostic task outlined below.

1. Understanding this Self of Yours

Please take some time to reflect on the kind of "stories" which you need to tell yourself about yourself, what sort of person you are.

When I have used the above exercise on retreats the great majority of participants have referred to a strong sense of *lack*, of personal inadequacy in shaping their dominant story. Each was surprised and moved to discover that they shared much the same feelings with everybody else. From our first experience of meditation, when we go in search of a still mind, we discover that our self feels threatened by that stillness. It struggles to maintain a strong sense of presence, even if this is reduced to endlessly ruminating over matters of no significance. Our self needs to feel active and doing, to feel a secure and enduring self identity.

At birth each of us is dealt a different hand in the extent and character of our self-neediness: we are each born with a different start in life. This depends on heredity and karmic rebirth (if you believe it), but also in our very first months of life and maybe even our experience in the birth canal. D.W. Winnicot, the pioneering paediatrician, maintained that many people suffer because of failure to receive sufficient parental support and affirmation in infancy. This is needful, because in the earliest stages of emotional development, before the development of something that could be called an autonomous ego, very severe anxieties may be experienced. Without an adequate parental environment in these early years some people feel, deep down, a strong sense of existential lack. In adulthood, self-centred, they clamour for attention and emotional recognition (love?) and may become punitive if they do not get their way. This may be so acute as to translate into a psychotic condition, with clear bodily manifestations. (See D.W.Winnicott, *Babies and their Mothers*, 1988, pp36−38, and also the Buddhist psychologist, Mark Epstein, *The Trauma of Everyday Life*, Penguin, 2013, pp29, 46).

At the other end of the spectrum are those relatively few who appear to have been born at ease with themselves and others. These are the easy people to work with, since they do not burn with the smoke of a self-centred agenda which obscures the task in hand and has to be negotiated before it can be readily addressed. The majority lie somewhere between these two extremes. Given favourable conditions they may get by in life for the most part. Finally there are the relative few who undertake a spiritual search, perhaps because just getting by is not good enough or even tolerable. I recall it was Jung who observed that to commit seriously to a spiritual practice it was necessary to be something of a neurotic.

What is the origin of this sense of existential inadequacy which marks our human condition? Let us go back to Buddhist basics. First there are the Three Signs of Being: Impermanence, Insubstantiality (of the self and of all phenomena), and Suffering. In the face of these the fearful self struggles somehow to find a solid and enduring identity, and a freedom from the pain caused by the lack of it. These struggles, cumulated down the centuries, have kept our world ablaze, as the Buddha exclaimed in his famous Fire Sermon: "All is burning... burning with the fire of greed, with the fire of hate, with the fire of delusion."

The Buddha and all the great Buddhist teachers have focussed attention on the self — your very own self — as lying at the heart of Buddhist practice — the Great Way, which leads to liberation from suffering and a self profoundly at ease with itself and all that is other. "To study Buddhism is to study the self; to study the self is to forget the self; to forget the self is to be enlightened by all things", proclaimed Master Dogen.. (It is unprofitable here to get entangled in the ancient debate as to what sense there is and is not a self. It is more helpful to understand the self as a process, as explained in the *skandha* theory of Buddhist psychology).

Note that Buddhism is not a spiritual anaesthetic for the pain of a broken leg or a broken heart. Buddha did not teach the way out of pain but the way out of *dukkha*, rather misleadingly translated as "suffering". In the *Sigalavada Sutta* he explains that when misfortune strikes we commonly experience what we feel to be a single sensation — "pain". In fact there are two feelings: first there is physical or emotional pain, but, secondly, there is also how we respond to that pain. For example it is well known that by changing our emotional response to a physical pain we can modify its acuteness. There are many common examples of the working of the two arrows, as in a hospital ward where all the patients broadly speaking experience the same pain, but the range of responses may vary widely, from abject depression to a cheerful concern for others.

Can you recall any experience of this kind from your own life?

The two arrows are important to bear in mind in emotional awareness practice since it is our distanced and conscious awareness of our response to the painful experience that is crucial, as opposed to being heedlessly engulfed by the sensation itself.

2. The Needy Self at the Heart of Buddhist Practice

That great twentieth century sage Krishnamurti once strode onto the stage before a large and expectant audience. He raised his arm and displayed the gap in his open hand between his thumb and his index finger. "Ladies and gentlemen, all the miseries of the world are to be found in that gap!" He displayed the misery created by desire and aversion — desire which can never be adequately satisfied to bring peace to the needy self, and aversion to what can never be adequately evaded. Or, as the Zen saying has it, we are all fleas on the hot griddle of life: the fleas that jump must fall and the fleas that fall must jump. Each of us has evolved our own unique pattern of feelings, thoughts, and behaviours to shape our lives in an attempt somehow to adapt to this predicament. Our griefs, afflictions and discomfitures range from losing our dearest, losing the respect of friends and co-workers, to losing our bunch of keys or getting tooth ache.

However, before we each explore and open in full awareness to our unique needy self two explanations will be helpful.

Neediness choice vs objective choice As we deepen our emotional awareness we are better able to distinguish between those objective choices which are simply necessary to living our lives, and choices which are driven by the existential neediness to which Krishnamurti refers. The former constitute a simple *duality* between this and that. The latter *dualisms* are made more to sustain and affirm our sense of self-identity than to reflect objective differences. There is, of course, no clear distinction between these two kinds of choice; in most cases there is something of both motivations. However, as our emotional awareness develops, our understanding and discrimination between the two sharpens.

Consider a meeting of a committee whose members must make decisions about the questions posed by an agenda. Hopefully there will be at least two or three members who are not so swayed by a subjective neediness to the extent that their objective assessments are significantly distorted. But there will usually be others who bring their own personal "agenda" to the table. They may feel a strong need to stamp their *own* decisions on the meeting (and like to hear their voice doing it). Or they may need to be liked and well regarded by other members, or perhaps their precarious self just wants to go along with the majority. A group whose work is dominated by the personal agenda of its members may become dysfunctional — brought to a standstill by what are called "personality problems".

Again, there are those who are distressed by the suffering in the world and commit themselves to some social activism movement. But there will usually be other motivations at work, such as a desire to make their life meaningful, or the secure feeling of belonging to a righteous movement.

Can you recall an episode in your own life where your decisions and choices were influenced by a subtle self need which you may not have fully recognised at the time?

The tech fix mentality and culture. Our modernist culture is marked by a great number of discomfitures which can be more or less remedied "out there", by the immense scientific and technical resources we have developed and deployed. If you have tooth ache a painless dental remedy is only a phone call away. If depressed, a medication may soon restore you to your usual good cheer. In short, we can now get more of this that we want, and less of that which we don't want, than ever before. Previously our hope lay in changing the experience of our affliction (the second arrow) through spiritual belief and practice. Hence the contemporary waning of religions of divine deliverance.

Nonetheless a wide range of unfixable discomfitures (like death) remain. And more fundamentally, the insatiable need for an invincible sense of self cannot be remedied by any techfix, though consciousness-changing drugs may be able to do so for a time.

3. "Our Lifelong and Unwinnable Lawsuit with Reality" (Hubert Benoit)

You are now in a position to actualise Krishnamurti's dramatic gesture in terms of your own life, and to reflect on how it has been shaped by a neediness to acquire emotionally, cognitively, physically and behaviourally whatever might strengthen your sense of a strong self-identity, and, contrariwise, to evade everything that might threaten to undermine its solidity and permanence. Thus David Brandon refers to swallowing a long kebab of roles, actions and thoughts which only temporarily fill my emptiness." For the self is insatiable, and herein lies the origin of *dukkha* ("suffering"), arising from this seemingly endless frustrating evasion".

Please reflect on what Benoit's poignant metaphor might mean in terms of your own life. It is as if two old friends were to meet up after a long absence and ask each other: "Well, how has it gone for you?" I maintain that a profound exploration of our needy selves is an essential and fundamental task underlying our spiritual enquiry. Herein lies "The Great Matter" of Zen Buddhism, from which the work of existential liberation can fruitfully proceed.

So, as an ongoing practice, please jot down and build up your existential autobiography, in whatever way suits you. This work may be undertaken off the meditation cushion at any suitable time and place. However, it will be most fruitful on the cushion, when the mind has been allowed to fall calm and there is some clarity beyond chatter and rumination.

What have been the underlying neediness that have driven your life? Please focus on the inner experience, whilst at the same time noting the objective conditions which may have affected you. Avoid overmuch intellectual analysis, preferring a loose, playful and meditative kind of enquiry.

Pay attention not only to the emotional impulsions driving your life. Our emotional needs can powerfully shape our cognitive landscape, ranging from what we think about ourselves to the many different "stories" we tell ourselves about the world (with plenty of gratuitous help from our culture and, above all, the mass media). The Buddha gave considerable prominence to the role of such "views" in the shaping of each self.

Now consider all of the foregoing — emotional, cognitive and behavioural — in the different spheres of your life — family, intimate relationships, the place of friends and friendship, your career, workplace and the like; and your choice of leisure activities and what might lie behind it. Finally, characterise your overall lifestyle, and reflect on why it is as it is.

How have your inner life and its outward manifestations unfolded over the years? Have there been any particularly instructive and revealing episodes?

When affliction strikes we seek somehow to avoid it, each with our favourite evasions. For some its is escape into denial, anger, self-pity or blame — "It's all your fault!" Denial may be masked by somehow rationalising our misfortune, to take the sting out of it, concentrating our attention on the circumstances "out there" and the resources of our fix-it culture.

Finally, there is a wide choice of evasions and distractions available which are habitual and readily addictive. *What are yours?* Busyness is perhaps the dominant one in our culture — certainly for the professional middle classes. I DO, therefore I AM. Twitter, Facebook and other busyness made attractive by iPods, tablets and computers have vastly increased the opportunities for this obsession. We then complain that we have too much to do and too little time to do it in — but what would we do without it? Shopping (consumerism) must run a close second, and then there is the vast and variegated industry of recreational sex. Finally, in every culture there are consciousness changing addictions. Indeed, with good health, more than a bit of luck, and a skilful combination of evasions and addictions, a person can get through life tolerably well without having to bother about the spiritual search (which anyway can itself become something of an addiction).

4. Our Authentic Self

The foregoing is surely, however, only a grave half-truth as an explanation of personality and behaviour. Please pause and ask yourself what is missing.

What of spontaneous kindly laughter, perhaps? Or the no less selfless and spontaneous anger at ill-treatment of another? And in our impulse to help another in distress we are surely not invariably and solely moved by self-interest — as David Brandon put it in his classic book *Zen and the Art of Helping*, "the only way I can let you know I need your help is to insist on helping you". Or when Chekhov warned that if you see someone coming towards you with the fixed determination to help you or do you good, make off in all haste in the opposite direction.

And yet the helper may, no less, be moved by a compassionate fellow-feeling, rather than by a hungry need to inflate the self, feeling important and superior to the one who appears to need our help. And, above all, to feel virtuous. This aspect of the self is variously known as the Buddha Nature, Big Mind, Original Mind, and tathata-garbha in Sanskrit. These terms are reminders of who we really are at heart, when freed of our fearful needy self, when freed of ill-will and aggressiveness. These are manifestations of the delusion from which our practice is designed to free us, so that more and more we live our lives authentically.

Note that the foregoing is not an expression of two selves, top dog versus bottom dog, or even two "sides" of the self — the kind of dualistic thinking from which the practice is designed to free us. These are rather to be thought of as two tendencies, and which is uppermost will depend on maturity of practice and, especially, external factors such as upbringing.

For the most part our motives may be mixed and problematic. Beware of our capacity for self deception. — the lust to be good, kind, righteous and unselfish, with the ultimate assurance of being a strong and admired self. For most of us most of the time our underlying motives may be hard to distinguish, though this becomes easier as we become more familiar with our emotional selves.

I recall an interview with a young man employed by a computer company who was in doubt about seeking a particular promotion. On the one hand he was moved by the knowledge that he had a particular skill in getting people to work together (which was a problem for the company), which he could do much to alleviate from a more senior position, making for a happier and more satisfied workforce. On the other hand he realised that he was by no means indifferent to the higher status and pay which would follow promotion. In the end he trusted his intuition and went for the promotion. Often we cannot be sure that we are being moved by our authentic self, but it is worth remembering that being able to act boldly in circumstances of doubt and uncertainty is itself a mark of the authentic self, which does not anxiously cling to being sure of getting it right.

In emotional awareness practice most writers are agreed that there is no better field of practice than an intimate relationship (though not necessarily an erotic one) — and especially a long-term one. Once the initial passion has died down we may reflect on how far that attraction depends on our needy self needing the other, and how far the authentic self is moved by a spirit of loving generosity. It is around these polarities that the relationship will develop, for better or worse.

Periodic experiences of our authentic self — with varying intensities of authenticity, resemble those brief experiences which we call insights, or openings, which appear from somewhere else than our needy self, from a "Big Mind". A vivid example is the creative writer or artist visited by her Muse, or a physical activity, where the body is infused by an energy or skill greater than usual. Likewise we may experience our authentic skill on some days, rather than those more common days when the needy self is struggling against its "unwinnable lawsuit". We feel more at ease, calm and relaxed, even though there may be no obvious explanation such as a good night's sleep, but when the needy self has temporarily given up.

An emotion is not in itself necessarily good or bad. The anger we feel at the ill-treatment of another is surely a "righteous" response to a particular situation. This is different from the anger experienced when we feel affronted, diminished or otherwise denied in our self-identity. Secondly, it would be a mistake to assume there are two selves at war within us. There is only one self; when moved to a delusive rage or any other negative this is the same self that also has the potential to behave selflessly. Thus it is said that "the passions are our Buddha Nature". Thich Nhat Hanh explains as follows:

> Treat your anger with the utmost respect and tenderness because it is no other than yourself. Do not suppress it; simply be aware of it. Awareness is like the sun. When it shines on things they are transformed. If you destroy anger you destroy the Buddha, for Buddha and Mara [the Evil One] are of the same essence. Mindfully dealing with anger is like taking the hand of a little brother.

It will now be necessary to amend, perhaps quite strongly, the autobiographical profile of your needy self assembled in the previous exercise. For a start, you might select some situation in your life which is important to you, such as a relationship, and meditate and reflect on how far your feelings, thoughts and behaviours in this situation come forth from the delusive, needy aspect of your self and how far from the selfless, other-centred aspect. This you will probably find difficult. What is valuable here, however, is the exploration itself, rather than coming up with some kind of apportionment.

5. A Note on Morality and the Will

Morality — in the sense of how we treat others — lies at the behavioural heart of Buddhism, as in other world religions. Straightway we are enjoined to cultivate a variety of ethical precepts and "perfections" (*paramitas*). In Buddhism these are to be understood as intentions and endeavours rather than "commandments". However, the needy and fearful self is essentially self-ish, valuing its status in the high regard of others, to be seen assuredly as good, kind, and in the right, displaying its virtues often with masterly self-deception. However, its only resource in achieving this is the exercise of self-will and the attempted subjugation of at least the more manifest kinds of self-indulgence. For top dog to keep bottom dog down may require quite a brutal exercise of repressive will-power — the mortification of the flesh, and much else which dries out the marrow in our bones.

Simone Weil, a perceptive twentieth century mystic, warns us that in spiritual practice there are only two safe uses of will-power. The first is to make emergency stops ("Just don't do it!") and the second is to sustain our spiritual practice — though not to drive it.

Ultimately to the extent we live an authentic self we naturally and spontaneously manifest an authentic morality. An authentic self is not some distant dream but an any day potential and possibility. But some mindful intent and prompting is helpful. For example, on my retreats I employ a simple liturgy which includes the following quotation from Zen Master Dogen:

> Let go of and forget your body and mind; throw your life into the abode of the Buddha. When you do this without relying on your own power, you become released from life and death and become a Buddha. Do not immerse yourself in mental and emotional struggles. Refrain from committing evil. Neither be attached to life or to death. Be compassionate towards all beings. Honour that which is superior, but do not withhold sympathy from that which is inferior. Do not harbour rancour or greed. Do not be overly concerned with trivial matters, nor grieve over difficulties in your life. This is the Buddha. Do not search for the Buddha anywhere else (from the *Shoji*, trans. Kosho Uchiyama)

Relevant to all this is a well-known meditation (commonly guided) in which the meditator seeks to feel loving-kindness (metta) first to those close to her, then to those to whom she is indifferent, and finally to those towards whom she feels antagonistic. Many, though by no means all, claim that this "works well" for them. However, I do have a reservation that the feelings aroused must to some extent be behavioural and hence superficial, as compared with those which arise unprompted and spontaneous from our authentic self. Certainly meditation can be more effective where the guide invites the meditator to open in awareness to any resistance or forcing of the feelings evoked.

The position of situational versus literal ethics may be of interest. Most ethical problems, whether personal or public, tend to be tangled and complex, with the most beneficial course of action uncertain. (Just sitting on the fence also implies a decision). It is therefore necessary to accept that sometimes the wrong course of action may be determined, perhaps with disastrous results. This prospect requires courage on the part of the situational decision maker. But the small self, the needy self, values above all feeling right, and clings to literal interpretations of the ethical precepts. I am reminded of an anecdote in which one precept must be broken if another is to be upheld. To the huntsman, "The fox went that way" (which it did not), then the first precept against killing is upheld. But since a Noble Lie (as Plato would call it) has been told, because in fact the fox went this way, the fourth precept, against deceit, has been broken.

Literal decision making may give the decision maker a gratifying sense of rightness, but, in difficult situations, at the cost of the well-being of those affected. Consider the dilemma facing a peacekeeping force in the anarchic situation of some broken-backed state, where drug-crazed boy soldiers are running wild in an orgy of ethnic cleansing. Some kind of order must be established before any attempt at mediation or reconciliation is possible. To this end military intervention will be essential, and it will be difficult to avoid loss of life, but will almost certainly avert a humanitarian disaster.

I have the impression that most, if not all, prominent teachers are inclined to a situationist ethic — certainly in the West. Nor is this a problem which has arisen in the context of contemporary Buddhism. Back in the thirteenth century the great Zen Master Eihei Dogen wrote perceptively, as set out in Hee-Jin Kim's excellent *Eihei Dogen: Mystical Realist* (Wisdom, 2004, pp 221–229), from which the following is taken.

> [For Dogen] the moral values of good, evil and neutral do not exist in themselves or for themselves with any independent metaphysical status, because they were nothing more than the temporary configurations resulting from infinitely complex interactions of conditions." (224). Dogen: *The human mind is neither good nor evil. Good and evil arise with circumstances... (223); What is good and what is bad are difficult to determine (221); Good is understood differently in different worlds (222).* Thus "a perennial question in Dogen's thought was What particular course of action am I to choose here and now in this particular situation? Dogen himself was acutely aware of the enormous difficulties in answering the question" (222). And so "although 'not to commit evil' was the moral, as well as the transmoral, sensibility that was intrinsic to enlightenment... this did not imply denial of the human propensity for failure and guilt ... that is why we must constantly repent and be forgiven" (225–6).

6. Making Gold out of Straw: The Practice of Emotional Awareness

We are now in a position to move from the Buddha's diagnosis of the typical human condition to beginning the practice which can liberate us from it.

In 1989 Charlotte Joko Beck, a teacher who had broken away from a traditional Zen master, published a book entitled

Everyday Zen (though it is no less applicable to other Buddhist traditions). This proved to be a landmark book, which initiated the Everyday Buddhism movement in the West offering an alternative to the traditional Asian monastic tradition of practice. This is a practice, on and off the cushion, of deep emotional awareness, as far as possible in the body, of the great and small discomfitures and griefs typically experienced by Westerners in the course of their busy and stressful lives. Such a practice comes head-on against our deeply ingrained habit of evasion. So the first problem which needs to be surmounted is to appreciate the potential value of developing a positive response to our misfortunes.

"May all sorrows ripen in me"

So proclaimed the great bodhisattva Shantideva. An ongoing endeavour in the practice of all Buddhist traditions and, indeed, of most inner-path spiritualities, has been to ingrain in ourselves a positive attitude to all the misfortunes visited upon us. Thus, in the Tibetan tradition: "Grant that I may be given appropriate difficulties and sufferings on this journey so that my heart may be truly awakened."

Here is Hubert Benoit's forceful explanation: "If an humiliating experience turns up, offering me a marvellous chance of initiation, at once my mind strives to conjure up what appears to me to be in danger. It does everything to restore me to that habitual state of satisfied arrogance in which I find a transitory respite, but also the certainty of further distress. In short, I constantly defend myself against that which offers to save me; foot by foot I fight to defend the very source of my unhappiness."

This, by the Persian Sufi poet Rumi, is particularly eloquent:

"This being human is a guest house.

Every morning a new arrival.

A joy, a depression, a meanness,

some momentary awareness comes

as an unexpected visitor.

Welcome and entertain them all

even if they're a crowd of sorrows,

who violently sweep your house

empty of its furniture.

Still treat each guest honourably;

he may be clearing you out

for a new delight."

Such dynamic acceptance lies at the heart of all existential liberation.

How to Cultivate Emotional Awareness

As a steady round-the-clock practice, select some ongoing difficulty, affliction or pain in your life. It may range from some persistent irritation (like the domestic untidiness of your partner) to something much deeper (like a haunting sense of guilt). But avoid taking on an affliction which, for the present, may be too emotionally overwhelming. Susan Murphy, a remarkable Australian Zen Master, urges as follows:

> What is the sharpest fact in your life right now? Take a moment to consider your most haunting terror, your most persistent aggravation or relentless criticism of yourself, or a deep pain you have taken upon yourself. Feel it in your body. That terror, aggravation, shame or sadness is your dearest enemy... All your creative power for the Way is to be found right there... So turning that way is turning toward your true freedom... Such is the blessing to be found in a curse.

As a preliminary exploration, why not try the following?

Think of a difficulty, affliction or pain in your life. As you sense this affliction, how does it feel, and how affect your body? Holding the feeling carefully, begin to ask yourself these questions, listening inwardly for their answers.

1 How have I emotionally responded to this affliction so far, and how have I suffered from my response and reaction to it?

2 What does this problem ask me to let go of?

3 What difficulties, if any, am I having with becoming deeply aware of my emotional response to this affliction?

The essence of emotional awareness practice is to become intimately aware of how the pain feels — and particularly how it feels in the body. This is a psycho-somatic practice. Bring your attention to where the feeling is seated, as in the flushed face, the increased heart beat, the tightened belly, the clenched fists of anger. Breathe your awareness into that space (itself a healing practice). What colour is it? (I have always felt self-pity to be blue). And even, is there a distinctive smell about it?

There are many different ways to go deep into how it feels. When the mind quietens on your cushion, there is the gentle enquiry to yourself (or to a partner, changing roles every five or ten minutes): "Tell me, how does it feel?" Different approaches seem to suit different practitioners, according to personality and inclination. Keeping a journal dedicated to the practice works well for some.

Here is a forthright advocacy from Pema Chödron, one of the many distinguished teachers and writers on emotional awareness.

> If you grab every opportunity to work with your mind — at home, at school, at work — you'll end up with more chances to work with strong emotions than in one hour of sitting on your cushion with some vague

idea of 'meditation'. In fact, your practice of working directly with your mind moment to moment will be much more powerful, because it will really change your mainstream. When you recognise an emotion with mindfulness, and penetrate it with some recognition of the nature of mind, that process is self-transforming. There's nothing more you need to do. When you can work with your mind in this way, you will clearly see its effect, not just in you, but in your environment — on your family and on your community.

Joko Beck's book, *Everyday Zen*, is subtitled "Love and Work", and she maintains that our typical work situations offer a field for our emotional awareness practice second in value only to our intimate relationships of various kinds. It's one thing to do a job which we like to do and can do well. It's quite another matter if we don't like doing it, do it badly, and with someone we dislike. And how do we respond to criticism? Everyday work situations can have enough fire in them to have us inwardly screaming at the unfairness of it all.

A graphic and moving description of emotional awareness in practice will be found in Darlene Cohen's book *Turning Suffering Inside Out: a Zen Response to Living with Emotional and Physical Pain*. She writes:

> People sometimes ask me where my own healing energy comes from. How in the midst of this pain, this implacable slow crippling, can I encourage myself and other people? My answer is that my healing comes from my bitterness itself, my despair, my terror. It comes from the shadow. I dip down into that muck again and again and am flooded with its healing energy. Despite the renewal and vitality I get from facing my deepest fears, I don't go willingly when they call. I've been around that wheel a million times: first, I feel the despair, but I deny it for a few days; then, its

tugs become more insistent in proportion to my resistance; finally, it overwhelms me and pulls me down, kicking and screaming all the way. It's clear I am caught, so at last I give up this reunion with the dark aspect of my adjustment to pain and loss. Immediately, the release begins: first peace, then the flood of vitality and healing energy.

7. Meditation and Acquisitveness

Please take time to reflect on what your current practice (if any) amounts to...

In the interviews I have conducted on retreats in a variety of different centres with newcomers I often begin by inquiring what their practice is. The reply is usually "meditation". And usually what this amounts to is periodic sitting with the aim of inducing "a peaceful mind". Beyond that, off the cushion, the practice commonly is described as "awareness" or "mindfulness". On closer enquiry this is at the level of "mindful dish-washing" and other relative superficialities of everyday life. Though not to be despised these go nowhere deep enough to turn around an ingrained consciousness. In addition, the student typically attends a week-long meditation retreat once or twice a year. This indeed settles the mind, but a few months later she usually claims to be back in much the same state of mind as before.

Nonetheless, periodic sitting meditation is an invaluable resource if well rooted in the totality of the practitioner's life. As the mind quietens, like the ruffled surface of a lake, it becomes possible to discern the monsters that breed at the lower depths — but we do need to look deeply. We need to bear in mind in meditation the need to make some distinction, however minimal, between the two dimensions of *samatha* (mind calming, serenity) and *vipassana* (inquiry, illumination). Even in the practice of "just sitting" ("silent illumination", *shikantaza*), where these two dimensions seem most closely combined there needs to be some explicit awareness of each. Thus the great twelfth century Chan master Hongzhi observed that "if illumination neglects serenity then aggressiveness appears ... If serenity neglects illumination, murkiness leads to wasted Dharma." Ajahn Chah, a celebrated teacher in the Thai forest monastery tradition, remarked that some of us are more skilled in one, others in the other, but he reassured his students not to be anxious about this, since a weakness in one dimension could be compensated by a strength in the other. *Which way round are you?* But note that an adequate competence does need to be cultivated in both modes.

Meditation is a bodily yoga. The basic position is important, whether on chair or cushion The vertebrae should stack up on a slightly forward tilted pelvis; chin in, eyes (lidded if possible) at forty-five degrees. Gently locked in place, this can be a very relaxed sitting position. In its long struggle to feel secure the self can embody a lot of tenseness. So, to settle down, turn your awareness to areas of tension, dropping the shoulders, letting out the belly, allowing the breathing to be natural, and so on.

It is usually best to begin with an all-body awareness check, and then give some time for the mind to settle down into bare awareness of just whatever is being experienced. Awareness of the body can provide an anchor for attention and stronger attention foci are available, of which awareness of, and counting, the breaths are the most common. As the mind quietens some gentle enquiry can be ventured. This should resemble the playful cast of an angler's rod, and should avoid falling into any kind of analysis. The self, if not quietened enough, is all too ready to get back and take charge! One helpful emotional awareness practice is gently to enquire "How does it feel?"

Everything this self of ours does is aimed at aggrandising and enhancing its sense of identity and purpose. We may therefore need to revise the whole conceptual vocabulary of what we are up to in the meditation hall, to dissipate the miasma of expectation which too often clouds it. (For more on this, click on *Unlearning Meditation* on www.kenjoneszen.com)..

It is particularly important not to see our meditation as an anxious struggle to will away thoughts as pernicious intruders disrupting "authentic" meditation, like swotting mosquitoes. To do so actually strengthens our goal-oriented sense of purpose. So long as we are aware of our day-dreaming it ceases to be day dreaming. Moreover some thoughts which arise may have something useful to say, such as the stories we tell ourselves about ourselves, and, more generally, to deepen awareness of the presence of the anxious self, crying out for attention and recognition.

If it is not locked into the emotional ups and downs of everyday life, sitting meditation can become something of a fetish, an obsession, for modern-day Westerners, especially in Zen, inspired by the round-the-clock spiritual athletics of monastic specialists. Indeed, the whole problem of practice arguably amounts to freeing oneself from the ingrained and deluded mentalities which are unknowingly brought to the practice. It is this that Chögyam Trungpa referred to in his invaluable book *Cutting through Spiritual Materialism.*

Understandably the beginner sees spiritual practice much as if she were, for example, learning to play a musical instrument. Central is the need to master some kind of technique (meditation). This requires a sustained effort, guided by a teacher, and extending over a period of time, and costing time and money. This prospect appeals strongly to our go-getting individualistic culture. Our spiritual practice readily becomes a specialism, with only limited transferability to our everyday life — a condition referred to as "spiritual bypassing". This readily breeds "spiritual inflation", particularly in an institutionalised hierarchy buttressed by the authority of a "master".

The acquisitive spirit may sometimes actually be reinforced by the teacher with metaphors like "breaking down the Dharma gate" or "climbing a glass mountain". Presumably this is designed to build up the student's frustration to breaking point, so that she realises the absurdity of her acquisitive mentality. What is in fact a sudden release of tension can produce an insight for which large claims may be made. Such an approach, which I endured myself for several years, with hindsight I would certainly not endorse,

Contrariwise there are many warnings from Zen teachers, ancient and modern, about the essential need for one's practice to be cleansed of any trace of acquisitiveness. Thus, Master Dogen:

> If you wish to practice the way of the Buddha ... you should expect nothing, seek nothing. Cut off the mind that seeks and do not cherish a desire to gain the fruits of Buddhahood. (*Zuimonki*)

And from Shunryu Suzuki:

> Whether you practice *zazen*{sitting mediation} or not, you have the Buddha nature. Because you practice it there is enlightenment in your practice. The point we emphasize is not the stage we attain, but the strong confidence in our original nature and the sincerity of our practice... according to Bodhidharma's understanding, practice based on any gaining idea is just a repetition of your karma. Forgetting this point, many late Zen masters have emphasized some stage to be obtained. We do not slight the idea of attaining enlightenment, but the important thing is this moment, not some day in the future. (*Zen Mind, Beginner's Mind*, 99–101).

The question remains however (and it was one which deeply concerned Master Dogen), that if the acquisitive urge is reduced to no more than an instructive example of needy self behaving as is to be expected, and simply noted and ignored, then how is the practitioner to be adequately motivated?

In my experience some reflection on our authentic self can be valuable here. If we have some intimation that, already, and manifested for at least some of the time, we are already "enlightened" we can approach our meditation with curiosity (rather then anxiety) and with a blend of playfulness and spaciousness. There is then no such thing as a "failed" meditation (and certainly not a successful one), only a failure to meditate at all. He or she who can accept themselves — wholeheartedly and with relief — as a meditation failure has made a great stride forward in their practice. Part of this, of course, is that they continue their sitting and learn from it.

The great Chan poem "Faith in the Heart" (*XinXinMing*) offers much encouragement to this radically different approach to our practice, as in these two passages:

The Great Way is calm and large hearted:

for it, nothing is difficult, nothing hard,

small and partial views are uncertain and insecure;

sometimes assertive, sometimes vacillating.

When you are not attached to anything,

all things are as they are (Arthur Waley, translator)

More encouraging still (and included in my home-made retreat liturgy) is the following as translated by Alan Watts):

Follow your nature and accord with the Way;

saunter along and stop worrying.

If your thoughts are tied you spoil what is genuine.

Do not be antagonistic to the senses;

when you are not it turns out to be complete awakening.

The wise person does not strive;

the ignorant tie themselves up.

if you work on your mind with your mind

how can you avoid a complete confusion?

The practice is thus a paradox — as is all that really matters in any spiritual endeavour, C. G. Jung reminds us. It is, as a favourite Zen koan has it, a "gateless gate". On the one hand, there does appear to be a gate. The practice really does require perhaps years of hard work, as time passes. But at the same time there really is no gate at all which we need to pass through. My favourite analogy is a learning-to-swim metaphor. At first, we follow the instructions, with arms, legs and breathing. But are disconcerted simply to find ourselves struggling and sinking, again and again. After a while I gave up on this and resigned myself to playing in the shallow end. And then, one day, I found myself floating, and from there it was a short and easy transition to swimming.

8. Suchness, Faith and Liberation

Our concern is to awaken fully to our authentic self, to be wholeheartedly at ease with ourselves and with others, moved by a spirit of wisdom and compassion. Up to now we have been concerned with "the practice", with the needy *this* versus *that* of Krishnamurti, growing into Hubert Benoit's lifetime unwinnable lawsuit with reality.

Our attention now shifts to consider the fruit of all this. How does a crucial change in our consciousness occur? What is it that drives it?

In the Zen literature this shift is commonly associated with the sudden experience of *kensho* (translated as "enlightenment"). "Body and mind are dropped off" and perhaps for several hours the sense of a separate self disappears. There is the frequent assumption that the adept thus enters a permanent *state* of enlightenment. Yet it seems scarcely credible that such a substantial change in consciousness could be effected by a single insight, however profound. In this paper I use the term "enlightenment" only to signify a *state* of mind, not an event.

It appears, moreover, to be a relatively rare event, certainly as far as Westerners are concerned. It strikes regardless of how well practised is the beneficiary, and not necessarily only in Buddhism or indeed on any spiritual path at all. The following remarks by Dr John Crook, a Chan master of long experience, are noteworthy.

> I am beginning to see that we Westerners need a different emphasis from that generated by D.T. Suzuki [influential in the West for his emphasis on *kensho*. In brief, we need to seek wisdom more than enlightenment... I mean that although enlightenment experiences can provide the opening insights of Dharma, few of us can attain them – simply because the natural egotism of the Westerner gets in the way ...One can, however, train in wisdom. Meditation practice, retreat experiences, self-confrontation and encounters with teachers, the problems of life and our quest to manage ourselves all yield wisdom if one cultivates mindfulness of their meaning... Whether one can cultivate a selfless mindfulness and compassion or not – that is what matters. Whether such understanding can be used in wise judgements in worldly affairs – that, too, is what matters. (*Chan comes West* 39–40).

A much more common insight is that of so-called unity consciousness, where we experience ourselves as a part of, and at one with, the universe, opening out from our acute-angled self-centred vision. Dogen described this as follows: "When the self advances, the ten thousand things retire; when the self retires, the ten thousand things advance". Typically we believe that we need to disperse the clouds that cover the sun of enlightenment, not realising that this is the reverse of the truth, and it is the sun constantly trying to get through to us if only we would let it.

Thus Dogen maintained that all the things "out there" are continuously attempting to enlighten us, but we remain stubbornly within the "mind-forged manacles" (as Blake described it) of our narrow, self-protective consciousness. But there may be occasions when, if we happen to be more in our spacious, authentic self, when, of a sudden, a tree, say, breaks in upon us with its sheer *presence*, and we are held in awe.

Underlying all such experiences there is, I believe, a "wearing out of the sandal of *samsara* (suffering)". We become more deeply aware of the futility of Hubert Benoit's lifelong and unwinnable lawsuit with reality, and one day it dawns upon us, with a huge sense of release, simply to give up this wanting life to be this and not that. This profound sense of *acceptance* is a watershed experience in all spiritual awakening. But acceptance is, however, a deeply misleading word. For this is quite the opposite of some shoulder shrugging and defeated sense of resignation. Even "equanimity" fails to convey its heartfelt sense of liberation. This is said to be where "the real practice" begins. The great contemporary Zen teacher Shunryu Suzuki was explicit about this: "If you have great faith and great acceptance there is no need to worry about enlightenment. This may come along sometime as an optional extra; it doesn't matter." I can still recall my shock several decades ago, when profoundly attached to gaining the prize of enlightenment, I discovered that the great Zen Master Dogen had proclaimed that Zen Buddhism is the Buddhism of *faith*. Yet faith is another misleading term. It refers here to the inexplicable certainty that somehow things are basically okay, felt with the force of insight, "And all shall be well and all manner of things shall be well" as T S Eliot proclaimed in *The Four Quartets*, echoing the mystics down the ages. It contrasts with the previous stage of *belief*, where our Buddhism is only upheld by the rational consideration that it appears to confirm our own experience of life.

The "acceptance" to which I refer above is the acceptance of how things are, their *suchness* or just-how-it-isness. Something still may be good or its may be bad, but we no longer take it personally. It's just how things are. Such suchness (*tathata*) may be taken as synonymous with "emptiness" in Mahayana philosophy. It offers a useful experiential entry point to that elusive concept.

Before exploring further, however we must take note of those exceptional experiences where rock bottom despair and hopelessness force us to abandon our habitual wanting that things should be different than they are. "Father, father, why hast thou forsaken me?" was Christ's cry from the cross. For countless despairing people their despair has turned into an exhilarating acceptance when they finally hit rock bottom — the implacable suchness of just how it is. From Easterhouse, a huge squalid housing estate on the outskirts of Glasgow, Jeremy Seabrook reports the following example.

> Cathy Mc Cormack, a passionate woman in her thirties, is committed to the kind of radical change which is believed, in more fashionable areas, to have been struck from the agenda. She speaks with an energy and authority which comes from having known despair during the seven years that she and her husband Tony have been out of work "I was so broken by it that I felt there was no point in living. I wanted to go to sleep and never wake up again. Then one day something happened. It was a kind of awakening: almost a spiritual experience." Cathy realised that nothing was ever going to happen, that no one was going to rescue them. "I understood that my life is here in this place, and that no fantasy of escape would help. This is where

the wains must grow up and make their lives; here we must perish together."

Inspired by a new energy Cathy returned to the struggle, the movement began to gain ground, and in due course the flats were demolished and the family rehoused.

This is the archetype of the "broken-hearted warrior", inspired and empowered beyond conventional hope and expectation. This is the joy of self truly at ease, the slow opening to wisdom ripened over many years of practice, whatever might have been the momentary insights, great and small, along the way which have assisted the embedding of that ease. Yet neither is it some kind of spiritual terminus: "The Buddha is still practising with us" as is said in Zen.

For those who dwell in faith Blakes's windows of perception are cleansed and they are released into a new *spaciousness* beyond the confines of the securely armoured self. In his delightful introduction to koan work, *Bring me the Rhinoceros* John Tarrant tells the story of a Zen master who asks his disciple to bring him his rare and valuable rhinoceros fan. Alas, it has been broken. "Then bring me the rhinoceros" exclaims the master. In that time a rhinoceros must have seemed a huge and semi-mythical beast. Here it is an analogy for our Big Mind, released into a previously unimaginable empowerment of possibilities for the life we might make for our self.

Many live, or attempt to live, their lives, by analogy, in a settled urban zone of secure predictabilities, where the buses leave for the station every hour on the hour. But for many there lies a more spacious world of music, art, literature, athletics, dreams, and erotic passions. Most of this countryside, however, is still well signposted, with its rights of way. Beyond it lies, again, a trackless wild-ness, where we can no longer be sure where we are and the teachers may be "crazy clouds" like Ikkyu and Chögyam Trungpa — and the contamination of ego in scandal may present a threat. And finally there is the Buddhist collective subconscious, *alayavijnana*, with its saints and monsters. Of this Jack Kornfield, in his book *The Wise Heart: Buddhist Psychology for the West*, shares with us some of his profound and startling meditation experience.

Spaciousness releases us into *playfulness*, one of the most important — and delightful — of the Zen "perfections". Be wary of those earnest and serious folk whose self-preoccupations have dried out their playfulness. In this playfulness there is the *vividness* of a new found clarity, a *joy* which transcends mere happiness, and a new-found *energy*.

9. Everyday Suchness

In this section we shall explore the implications of suchness for how we live our everyday lives.

First, recall some situation in your life where you typically feel "if only it were different". Like, "if only I'd married somebody else"; "If only I hadn't landed myself in this dead-end job". Assume that leaving the situation would be worse than sticking with it. Try easing yourself into how it might feel to drop the gnawing desire that things should be different. How would it feel to accept wholeheartedly that, for "better" or "worse" this in fact is just how it is?

The following examples may help in sensing how suchness feels.

Of a significant person in our life, David Brandon wrote: "If only I could throw away my urge to trace my patterns in your heart." What we feel is whom we see and what we feel about them. We see them in our light, not theirs. If we see them in their suchness, of a sudden out of the corner of our eye, it can be a startling experience. Thus did Zen Master Dogen explain "Every creature covers the ground it stands on; no more nor no less, it never falls short of its completeness". To relate to the other in their suchness (instead of only what we like about them) is surely the essence of true love.

And what of our self, with all its weaknesses and inadequacies? Loving oneself can surely be the most difficult of all loves – and the precondition for truly loving others. How much better to be able to laugh with her or him at the next foolishness or failure, instead of trading blame and reproach. Here one's self as one's closest lifelong friend and companion, in this poem by Derek Walcott:

> The time will come
>
> when, with elation,
>
> you will greet yourself arriving
>
> at your own door, in your own mirror,
>
> and each will smile at the other's welcome
>
> and say, sit here. Eat.
>
> You will love again the stranger who was your self.
>
> Give wine. Give bread. Give back your heart
>
> to itself, to the stranger who has loved you
>
> all your life, whom you have ignored.

Seen above a Chan temple arch in Hong Kong: "There is no time; what is memory?" It stopped me in my tracks. Please consider what it means to you.

Time and the passage of time is another area where a sense of suchness can transform our experience. Our needy self struggles to solidify and control a threatening sense of the passage of time. Our letters, photographs, memories, diaries, and dreams, however, can exist nowhere but now, in the present. Our past is, in that sense, an illusion. Our future is a complete unknown, though our plans and diaries give the illusion of controlling it. And as to the present, it is gone no sooner than it arrives. Indeed, time itself has no tangible existence other than in the experience of being (which is itself impossible outside time). These ramifications have been explored with great subtlety by Master Dogen in a masterly essay "Being Time" (*Uji*).

Returning more explicitly to suchness, imagine a group of people of varying ages. There is nothing illusory about these differences in age, as witnessed by the wear of their bodies. But if we observe them in their suchness, beyond the this of youth and the that of age, there are neither young nor old; each is just as they are.

So it is with summer and winter. True, the first is hot and the latter cold. But if we don't put such comparative distinctions to them each is no more than how it feels, its suchness. Formally speaking, we have here two paradoxical truths. But when we become habituated at moving from duality to suchness and back, and living in both, life becomes for us more spacious and playful. This is particularly so when we are struck by the second arrow of discomfiture, as described earlier. There are many koans and anecdotes to help us live lightly in this way. What do you make of this one? High in the mountains there is an old pond: shallow or deep, no one has seen to the bottom? Eschew grinding down your logical teeth; instead, enjoy the wondrous, playful spaciousness of that old pond. And, next time misfortune strikes, could it just be a case of "sun-faced Buddha; moon-faced Buddha"?

Finally, let us return to the workplace. Suppose your boss has told you she wants a particular report from you on her desk by noon. But you know that you have much too little time to do adequate research and produce a report which adequately demonstrates your expertise. Momentarily, you may even revert to your old mentality of longing for that, rather then being restricted to this. However the suchness of the circumstances is unavoidable, and you take it lightly and clear-headedly. And so, whatever its inevitable limitations, the resulting report will doubtless be superior to one written in a frustrated sense of injustice.

10. Inclusive Buddhism

In all religious traditions there have been sages who remained trapped in the bliss of "all things being well." They have never come down from the mountain into the market place. Buddhism in particular has been reproached for a mystical quietism, which is quite a common view of the religion. Even the great Chan scripture the *XinXinMing* ("Trust in theHeart") tends to be flawed in this respect — as in the half-truth "Profit and loss, good and bad, away with them once and for all." Yet how can all manner of things be well when the world, as the Buddha proclaimed in his Fire Sermon is ablaze with greed, hatred and delusion? There is evidently a major paradox here — which has been laboriously termed "The Doctrine of the Two Truths." Fortunately it can be readily enough understood, though feeling it and living it is another matter... The best explanation I know is that of R.H.Blyth, which I have adapted as follows:

> Things may be hopeless
>> but not dispiriting;
> unjust
>> but not hateful;
> beautiful
>> but not desirable;
> loathsome
>> but not rejected.

Note how the paired attributes are carefully chosen to distinguish between the typical responses of the fearful, needy and aggressive self on the right hand and on the other that of the authentic self at ease. The latter does not need to "take things personally", as if it were still engaged in its unwinnable lawsuit. And if we are truly at ease with self and other, what else remains to be done but to be of service to others? This is the active compassion of the bodhisattvas, those mythic saints of Mahayana Buddhism, who could go down to hell to rescue all beings and yet treat it as if it were a fairground without any the less feeling for those suffering there. It was in the same seriously playful spirit that Oscar Wilde warned that the world was in too great a mess to be taken seriously.

Note that we are still here with the suchness of just-how-it-is, freed of the self-centred anxiety of how dreadful (for us) it is. More subtly, here is the testament of Norman Fischer, a fine Zen teacher, on the suchness of bereavement:

> I have experienced extreme sadness and loss, feeling the whole world weeping and dark with the fresh absence of someone I love. At the same time I have experienced some appreciation and equanimity, because loss, searing though it can be, is also beautiful, sad and beautiful. My tears, my sadness are beautiful because they are the consequence of love, and my grieving makes me love the world and life all the more. Every loss I have ever experienced, every personal and emotional teaching of impermanence that life has been kind enough to offer me, has deepened my ability to love.

To suppose that we have arrived at the participative Buddhism of the bodhisattva towards the *end* of our survey of the Great Way could be seriously misleading. The same might be said of the ox herding (or bull taming) sequence of pictures used in Zen teaching to illustrate the successive stages of the Way. For here it is not until the end that the sage comes down from the mountain into the market, "with bliss bestowing hands".

We have earlier emphasised that we should try to sense something of our authentic self from the very beginning of our practice. And since this is the self of active compassion it cannot but be engaged selflessly with the world out there. And the emotional awareness practice exposes us to all the discomfitures and griefs we encounter "out there", which the small self tries to deny or evade. An Everyday Buddhism cannot be anything other than a wholly inclusive one, focussing relentlessly as it does upon our doings in the world. Thus as early as the thirteenth century Zen Master Dogen, one of the outstanding figures in the history of Buddhism, maintained that "Those who regard worldly affairs as an obstacle to their training do not realise that there is nothing such as worldly affairs to be distinguished from the Way" (Bendowa, *Wholehearted Practice*). He would surely have been critical of what that pioneer Buddhist activist David Brandon mockingly called "mañana Buddhism" the view that social action should be delayed until enlightenment has been attained.

Inclusive or participatory Buddhism covers a broad spectrum; all human life is there. There are those for whom to bring up a family — or just to survive — is itself a harsh engagement on the scant incomes of a cruelly unequal society. Again, increased longevity means that many, no sooner had their children become relatively independent than they must care for elderly relatives — and such caring can be very demanding and self-sacrificing. At the other end of the spectrum is the social activism of "engaged Buddhism", about which I have written extensively (see my website).

For Dogen the world is alive with variant perceptions and possibilities, and hence the bodhisattva spirit of serious playfulness. The Korean scholar Hee-Jin Kim writes of Dogen's emphasis on *dotoku* — active compassion as follows:

> In Dogen's view, things, events, relations were not just given, but were possibilities, projects and tasks that can

be acted out, *expressed, and understood as self-expressions and self-activities of the Buddha-nature* [my italics — KJ]. This did not imply a complacent acceptance of the given situation but required man's strenuous efforts to transform and transfigure it. Dogen's thought involved this element of transformation, which has been more often than not grossly neglected or dismissed by Dogen students. (*Dogen Kigen: Mystical Realist*, p183).

Also, the first line of the quotation reminds us that there are "no things as they really are", only liberation from "I see what I am". Neither is there a "Pure Consciousness", a nirvana where there is security at last from the flux of impermanence and the pit of insubstantiality. On the contrary the bodhisattva finds true freedom in impermanence and insubstantiality and a world of infinite and wondrous possibilities.

The above contrasts with the narrow vision of the self which needs to find affirmation and reinforcement as a return for its good works out in the world — and especially a fetishism of *results*, as Christopher Titmuss called it. This was why the post-war Japanese peacemaker and activist Hisamatsu Shin'ichi devised for his followers the koan "If there is nothing you can do that is of any avail, what do you do?" This leads to what must surely be the ultimate koan for an inclusive Buddhism: "Nothing matters; Everything matters."

I invite you to reflect on how far your own life is, if at all, participatory beyond personal concerns which give your needy self some pay-back, however subtle.

How far, in the light of suchness, can you explain the koan? Can you illustrate it from your own life?

A Postscript

At the end of my retreats students ask me why mine is, for them, the first to deal at some length with a fully inclusive and participatory Buddhism, while others stopped short with some general reference to bodhisattvas?

There are historical reasons why Buddhism has traditionally been confined to individual existential concerns. Most of its traditions have been too economically dependent upon established authority to critique it and more inclined to endorse it. The bodhisattvas have arguably been more concerned in the long run, to "save all beings" rather than primarily remedying social ills.

Here, as elsewhere, Buddhist modernity has confined itself to the traditional Asian existential remit. Its historic tragedy has been its failure to emphasise a fully participative Buddhism, and in particular to explain how existential suffering translates into social and institutional suffering. The latter has been left to a handful of scholars like David Loy and myself. It is true that for many years there was indeed a flourishing, comprehensive and global socially engaged Buddhist movement, but two or three years ago it quite suddenly went into eclipse. It has been largely replaced by some single issue movements, more or less confined to originating sanghas, (like Thich Nhat Hanh's Community of Interbeing) and, above all by the rise of a mindfulness movement which is certainly no substitute for it.

Thus a socially engaged Buddhism has not become part of public discourse in the West, nor is there any Buddhist think tank dedicated to it. It has not created a significant body of "steady state" men and women who could challenge the dominant assumption that our concerns are exclusively societal, rather than originating ultimately in the kind of people we typically are. Buddhism, like other inner path religions, has demonstrated that this is a remediable condition. But until it is significantly remedied all attempts, in the face of a deepening global crisis, to create radically different social order will fail as they have done in the past. Gary Snyder's vision of a fusion of the existential (spiritual) revolution of the

44

East with the social revolutionary tradition of the West has sadly come to nothing. But I hope that, at the least, if enough of us can embrace an Everyday Buddhism better adapted to modernity, we shall make a better job of struggling on.

11. A Note on the Mindfulness Movement

The above concerns inevitably raise some fundamental questions about the burgeoning mindfulness movement, particularly in that on most retreats there are usually participants involved in it. It is also remarkable for the many and conflicting views which Buddhists seem to have about it.

The mindfulness movement originated in the work of Jon Kabat-Zinn, a well seasoned Buddhist as evident from his writings — and especially the splendidly titled *Full Catastrophe Living*. He is also an experienced clinician moved by the chronic unhappiness, verging on depression, of many of his patients. The bodily awareness programmes he conducted, and which depended much on the can-do spirit he inspired in his patients, proved remarkably successful, as "Mindfulness-Based Stress Reduction". Kabat-Zinn was concerned not to frighten the horses (and not least his professional colleagues) by making any explicit reference to the Buddhist origins of his work. And ever since Buddhism has for the most part been kept at arms length from the movement — and probably wisely.

In the UK National Health Service it has been adopted as a proven and inexpensive "talking therapy" for reducing the percentage relapse of patients treated for depression. It has been reinforced by Behavioural Therapy. However I have the impression that this has been not a significant addition.

Mindfulness is now widespread, particularly in America, extending to a wide spectrum of professions, organisations and activities which find it significantly enhances their effectiveness. They extend to politics, big business, the commercial media and even the military.

It reduces *stress* and, secondly, enhances *attention*, especially emotional self-awareness (though at a relatively superficial level compared to the practice described in this manual) — both in a society very needful of both. Within its limits its value has been and is being hugely effective, and its teaching and practice can be a considerable undertaking.

It also doubtless leads some to enquire more deeply about the Buddhism from which it sprang, and to which it comes close in what has been termed "Buddhism lite". This is a not particularly demanding lifestyle Buddhism found among the educated white middle class, akin to related fashions like yoga and veganism. The emphasis seems to be on *shamatha*, with the emphasis on stress relief and a more inwardly peaceful life. This is presumably the kind of Buddhism which the eminent sociologist Slavoj Zizek had in mind as "the opium of the middle classes", following Marx's religion as the opium of the people.

The mindfulness movement is thus essentially a *therapeutic* phenomenon contrasting with authentic traditional *existential* Buddhism, which is concerned with the human condition itself and with fundamental change in the kind of people whom we typically are. Buddhism goes down to the very roots of greed, aggression and ignorance which sustain so much in politics, big business and other centres of wealth and power in our society. Such a creed would hardly be welcome in Silicon Valley or the U.S. Marine Corps.

Mindfulness is thus typically a *technique* devoid of the profound ethical concerns of authentic Buddhism. For the ultimate concern of the Great Way, as we have seen, is our active compassion for the well-being of others — for all others — and an underlying awareness as to why we find this difficult.

46

An Overview of my Everyday Buddhism

Learning and practising Everyday Buddhism begins with some understanding and deepening awareness of Krishnamurti's dramatic gesture and Benoit's unwinnable lawsuit as illustrations of our needy self. This is based on an emotional awareness practice-in-the-body, both on and off the meditation cushion, of the ups-and-downs, the griefs and discomfitures of each our everyday lives. But from the start this needs to be combined with some sense of our authentic self, our underlying compassionate self. This lightens, and eventually eliminates, the urge to acquisitiveness and replaces it with a growing playful spaciousness. There is increasingly a liberative acceptance of things just as they are, in their *suchness*, a "faith" that somehow all is well with ourselves and the world. Beyond this lies a deepening of the inclusive and participative nature of mature Buddhism, which is in fact present from the very start of our practice of the Great Way.

All this can, in my experience, be effectively taught on a five day retreat, maintaining good cheer and high morale among the students, with plenty of fun. But there will, of course, be much less sitting meditation than on a conventional retreat which may contain little else. However, it may better suit a teacher's personal style to focus on one or two particular topics, so long as the retreat participants are left also with some sense of the overall Great Way.

The essence of the retreat's teaching has been wonderfully expressed by William Blake in his *Auguries of Innocence*:

Man was made for joy and woe;

and when this we rightly know

through the world we safely go.

Joy and woe are woven fine,

a clothing for the soul divine.

Under every grief and pine

runs a joy with silken twine.

A Liturgy

I give below the daily liturgy with which I ended up after much experimentation. It is designed to highlight features of the retreat, and to be cheerfully accessible to retreat participants who may never have experienced this kind of thing before. I eventually jettisoned the Heart Sutra which is really much too sophisticated in its presentation for the kind of retreat on offer here. The Guanyin mantra requires a bit of practice; my colleague Hilary Richards has an audiotape.

OUR INTENT

1 — Opening Invocation

NAMO BUDDHAYA

NAMO DHARMAYA

NAMO SANGHAYA

NAMO NAMA

OM

AH

HUM

2 — Chant of Atonement

All evil karma ever committed by me since of old

on account of my beginingless greed, anger and ignorance

born of my body, mouth and thought

now I atone for it all

3 — Master Dogen's Resolution (from the *Shoji,* trans. Kosho Uchiyama)

> Let go of and forget your body and mind; throw your life into the abode of the Buddha. When you do this without relying on your own power, you become released from life and death and become a Buddha.
>
> Do not immerse yourself in mental and emotional struggles. Refrain from committing evil. Neither be attached to life or to death. Be compassionate towards all beings. Honour that which is superior, but do not withhold sympathy from that which is inferior. Do not harbour rancour or greed. Do not be overly concerned with trivial matters, nor grieve over difficulties in your life. This is the Buddha. Do not search for the Buddha anywhere else.

4 — Guan Yin Mantra

> BO-SA NÂMU GUAN SHI YIN

5 — "Trust in the Heart" *(XinXinMing);* a passage on our authentic nature, as translated by Alan Watts.

> Follow your nature and accord with the Way;
>
> saunter along and stop worrying.
>
> If your thoughts are tied you spoil what is genuine.
>
> Do not be antagonistic to the senses;
>
> when you are not it turns out to be complete awakening.

The wise person does not strive;

the ignorant tie themselves up.

If you work on your mind with your mind

how can you avoid a complete confusion?

6— The Precepts (Version by David Evans)

Recollecting Gautama Buddha and all his true heirs, we take refuge in this teaching and in those who follow it with us.

We seek to practice and promote:

Compassion for all living things;

Non-violence and justice in human affairs;

Truthfulness and goodwill in speech and writing;

And a middle way for all beyond privation and greed.

May we be mindful of the transience of life, the suffering in the world, and the triviality of self, now and when we go forth.

Completed by three deep bows, symbolising our laying down of the needy self.

Reading List

BECK, Charlotte Joko *Nothing Special: Living Zen*(Harper-Collins, 1993).

BAYDA, Ezra *Being Zen: Bringing Meditation to Life*(Shambhala 2003). This, and the succession of other titles Bayda has written since then, are strongly recommended.

BRANDON, David *Zen and the Art of Helping* (Routledge & KP, 1976). A classic must— never out of print!

COHEN, Darlene *Turning Suffering Inside Out: A Zen Approach to Living with Emotional and Physical Pain*(Shambhala, 2002). Outstanding – quirky, outrageous, wise and unputdownable!

JONES, Ken *The New Social Face of Buddhism* (Wisdom, 2003).

KORNFIELD, Jack *Bringing Home the Dharma: Awakening Right Where You are* (Shambhala, 2011). More advanced (but not to be missed) is his 400-page book *The Wise Heart* (Rider, 2008) – a veritable treasure house of. Buddhist practice.

LOY, David *Money, Sex and War: Notes for a Buddhist Revolution.*(Wisdom, 2008).

LOY, David *The World is Made of Stories* (Wisdom, 2010).Wonderfully stimulating!

MURPHY, Susan *Upside-Down Zen – Finding the Marvellous in the Ordinary* (Wisdom, 2006). Highly insightful and poetic approach which usefully complements Bayda and Kornfield.ROTHBERG, Donald *The Engaged Spiritual Life: A Buddhist Approach to Transforming Ourselves and the World*(Beacon Press, 2006). Powerful and closely written, with lots of useful exercises.

TARRANT, John *Bring me the Rhinoceros* (Shambhala, 2004). A delightful introduction to working with koans.

VAJRAGUPTA *Buddhism: Tools for Living your Life*(Windhorse, 2007). British, aimed at beginners, but with a wide scope and lots of DiY exercises.

WELWOOD, John, *ed. Ordinary Magic: Everyday Life as Spiritual Path* (Shambhala 1992). (35 extracts)

Eight Retreat Talks

This is a series of writings which encapsulate talks given on various retreats, and which now more resemble "chapters". Several of the originals were not recorded at all or else have been recorded in different locations, with much overlap, and with all the disadvantages of unedited, ad hoc records. They provide an expansion of the above "manual" "How to Do Everyday Buddhism," with some unavoidable repetition of key quotations and the like. This series is produced in response to several requests for a more permanent and edited record than direct recordings, for distribution to past retreatants on my mailing list and to anyone else whom I believe might find them interesting. They are freely available for circulation elsewhere, with due acknowledgement.

Talk One — The Lifelong Lawsuit against Reality

We must begin with how we actually experience our life. And more particularly by enquiring what it is that moves us to undertake Buddhist practice. Unfortunately our concern may be rather abstract and distanced from our self, like, what is the meaning of life? Or it may be posed in objective terms, pointing away from the self, like, why is there something terribly wrong with the world? Or, more subtly, how can this self achieve the prize of "enlightenment"?

We may fail to appreciate that, since Buddhism is about how we *experience* the difficulties in our life, then our inquiry must be directed inwards, into who or what is doing the inquiring? This was emphasised by Zen Master Dogen, one of Buddhism's greatest monk-philosophers:

> To study Buddhism is to study the self;
>
> to study the self is to forget the self;
>
> to forget the self is to be enlightened by all things (1).

Meditation

To be able to pursue our inquiry with clarity it is essential that we become experienced meditators.

Meditation is not a means by which the self can make itself calm and tranquil. Meditation is about the cultivation of awareness, not a peaceful mind. With awareness, the latter will appear in its own time, and not by some act of will. Indeed, an excellent time in which to meditate is when our mind is agitated and even in turmoil, for at such times we can observe with greater clarity its struggles to escape its discomfiture.

It is true that if we can develop a calmer mind we may indeed be able to live without such artificial aids as Prozac, and be less easily provoked to anger by others. We may feel that our meditation has accomplished what it is supposed to do. In fact, Buddhism has never claimed that calming the mind is itself the means of resolving suffering in our life; calming the mind is not the same as transforming the mind. It is rather that the calm mind of *samatha* meditation is essential for enabling us to observe (in *vipassana* meditation), our emotional dynamics, and the physical changes which accompany them, the better to transform the way in which we customarily experience living our life. Thereby, in William Blake's words we "cleanse the [windows] of perception". When the waves of mental agitation no longer obscure the surface, we can observe the creatures that breed at greater depth…

There are many warnings in Buddhism about the dangers of becoming attached to the profound calm of *samatha* and the bliss of a state of trance. Ajahn Chah, a celebrated meditation teacher in the Thai Forest Tradition of Theravada Buddhism, has observed that "one could sit for two hours or even all day, but the mind doesn't know where it's been or what's happened. It doesn't know anything There is calm, but that's all. It is like a well sharpened knife which we don't bother to put to any use. This is a deluded type of calm because there is not much self-awareness" (2). However, we must at least establish "a modicum of tranquillity and one-pointedness of mind. Then you can use this to examine yourself. Nothing special is needed. If absorption comes in your practice this is okay too. Just don't hold onto it" (3). Ajahn Chah adds that some people may not have the capacity to develop deep tranquillity but that, if of a reflective state of mind, they may nonetheless open to wisdom. Calm and insight thus go together to give insight into wisdom and compassion.

Illumination will not come to us through thinking; it will not come to us through not thinking. In our meditation on the self and its emotional dynamics we shall not see clearly if we eschew all inquiry. Neither shall we if we pursue our inquiry with a self-conscious concern driven by our neediness, creating a dualism between self and the elusive object of inquiry. Bright and alert, with bare awareness we allow ourselves to settle into a calm frame of mind and playful inquiry, light as a feather. This is a wide open awareness in which we feel our emotions, hear our thoughts, and experience our bodily sensations. Chögyam Trungpa distinguished it from the acquisitive mentality which waits to pounce on emergent thoughts like a cat at a mouse hole.

For acquisitive Westerners meditation can too easily become a fetish, reduced to being the "technology of enlightenment". It can become just something else that Buddhists "do", something else to be somehow slotted into a busy schedule, and tarnished with the mentality of purposive busyness. Much to commend are times of mindful idleness, where the self is not affirmed by doing anything at all. How does that feel?

The Lawsuit

Sitting in meditation we may vividly experience the constant agitation of our self, anxiously proclaiming "Yes, I'm here! — alive and kicking!" From what black hole is it struggling to escape? There is evident here a sense of existential insecurity, a deep seated unease, an inner emptiness, a sense of lack. This precariousness finds expression in the best of our literature, of which the following by Joseph Conrad, a novelist of particular interest to Buddhists, is a good example:

> Life knows us not and we do not know life — we don't even know our own thoughts. Half the words we use have no meaning whatever and of the other half each man understands each word after the fashion of his own folly and conceit. Faith is a myth, and beliefs shift like myths on the shore; thoughts vanish; words, once

pronounced, die; and the memory of yesterday is as shadowy as the hope of tomorrow (4).

The Buddha traced this angst to the Three Signs of Being: Insubstantiality, Impermanence, and *Dukkha*. The last is the suffering arising from the ultimately unavailing struggle to consolidate and experience a sense of self, sufficiently strong and enduring to deny the insubstantiality and impermanence of all phenomena, including us. This has been characterised as a lifelong and unwinnable lawsuit with reality.

The fragility of self impels us to grasp at whatever may strengthen it and to reject whatever threatens it — hence the "Three Fires" of acquisitiveness, rancour, and existential ignorance. When the mind is sufficiently still we can readily sense the constant pull of desire and aversion, likened in Zen to fleas on a hot griddle: "the fleas that jump must fall, and the fleas that fall must jump".

It is a valuable part of our transformational practice to recollect our own distinctive lawsuit — our ingrained and habituated response to our human condition over the years of our life. In this way we can each write our own existential autobiography, with which we need to become intimate — however reluctantly! Each of us will have been dealt a different hand — by genetic conditioning, by upbringing, and (if we choose to believe it) by the karmic transmutation of past lives. Some may find themselves to be so vulnerable and fearful that their life appears as a record for the most part of quiet desperation. Exceptional people at the other end of the spectrum may have experienced a life substantially at peace with themselves, and barely casting a shadow of self-need upon the world.

It is important that our existential autobiography should not be a pseudo "Buddhist" caricature of the life we have lived. For Buddha Nature is in fact the ground of our being — a naturally wise and compassionate disposition, to which we seek to awaken and which is typically clouded and distorted by "the fires" of our existential fear. Consider, for example, the commonly mixed motivation in an urge to help others. On the one hand we may be moved, more or less, by an authentic spirit of selfless compassion. But this may be mixed with feelings of self-importance, in virtuously assisting another person who is in some sense inferior to us. Similarly, in seeking a more senior position in an organisation our motives may include the matter-of-fact that we do need higher pay in order to support our family the better; that we have talents the exercise of which would fulfil our potential and would be of benefit to others; and thirdly (and maybe not least) promotion would give a prestigious boost to our sense of self. Only if we have cultivated a certain detached clarity of mind is it possible to tease out the different impulsions which go to shaping our life.

Inquiry

Our "lawsuit" is conducted on several levels: (a) it is driven by ingrained emotional patterns, including our favourite kinds of evasion in the face of life's discomfitures; (b) these will in part generate views and attitudes through which we make sense of our life and our world, and of which we may be more, or less, aware; (c) behavioural patterns, as exemplified, say, in our preferred lifestyle. For example, a strong sense of insecurity may translate into assumptions that people tend to be undependable and not to be trusted, and this in turn may lead to a closed-off attitude to life.

All the above "levels" are acted out in different spheres of a life — in the wider world of work, leisure and our public persona; in the intimate world of relationship between spouses, children and parents; in our responses to the passing of time and to our ageing; in our relationship to "my body"; and finally and most fundamentally, in our relationship with this self itself which encompasses all the other spheres.

Moreover the distinctive ways in which we confront life and try to come to terms with it are enacted in much the same way in the different spheres of our life. Essentially we are the same person at home, at work, at play — in our public and in our private persona (though this may not always be evident on a superficial plane).

In recollecting in this way our life story and our present situation this, our Dharmic autobiography, reveals the characteristic of our Dharmic personality, that is, our personality as perceived in the light of a Buddhist understanding and as the indispensable subject of reflection and awareness at the heart of our practice. A variety of inquiry strategies will be found in the books comprising the reading list attached to these notes. The following exercise has been adapted from one in Vajragupta's book *Buddhism: Tools for Living your Life* (5):

> How the self struggles to inflate and defend itself — tossed between *Desire* and *Aversion* as in the following three realms:

A — Between *Pleasure* and *Pain*

We may, for example, experience much restlessness and dissatisfaction and a longing for the highs, for the red letter days, as being what our life is really about. Physical and emotional pain we commonly evade in many different ways, like denial, rationalisation, objectification, projection and self-blame.

B — Between *Gain* and *Loss, Fame* and *Blame*

The driven lust for gain is possessive of things, experiences, people, time, role and position, and health. All these can strongly upholster our precarious sense of self. Even an insignificant loss may be obsessively magnified in that it is felt as a loss of control by the self over its world, grounded on the endemic sense of inadequacy which many of us appear to feel.

As to fame, we may be anxious above all to be liked and accepted. We may observe ourselves jostling for attention. Conversations may become competitions, with people hardly waiting for the last person to finish before they jump in with a joke or anecdote that trumps what has just been said. We may feel put down even by well merited criticism, and struggle to reject it without either attempting to understand and appreciate it or to examine where our instant denial is coming from.

C — Between *Aggressiveness* and *Fearfulness*

Many are moved by a strong sense of rancour, just waiting for some situation to turn up which will arguably justify its expression. Anger may be so near the surface that the person becomes known as having "a short fuse" before their ready explosion. Others have such a fragile sense of self that they are easily

> *Note:* In all three of the above it is the hungry self with which we are concerned here. It is with how phenomena are *experienced*, rather with the phenomena themselves. For example, if we have particular talents it is natural that to want to put them to good use and natural to welcome any recognition received.

Question One *Take each of the above pair of compulsions (A, B and C) in turn and try to recall at least two or three instances when you have been driven by them. Do you tend to be more affected by some of the above than by others? Which?*

Question Two *Can you identify in yourself any other ways in your life in which the self has sought to fortify itself and any other circumstances in which it feels it has been threatened?*

Question Three *Can you suggest strategies for dissolving these ego impulsions and living your life more freely and authentically?*

Beyond the above recollection-and-identification level of inquiry, however, lie the key awareness practices (prefigured in "Question Three" above) by means of which we can radically transform the way we experience living this life, enabling us to "turn straw into gold", as Jack Kornfield puts it. A later essay offers specific guidance for this work, focussed on "where the shoe pinches most", that is to say, on some acutely felt pain or discomfiture in our lives. This is a particularly powerful practice which I most favour for my Emotional Awareness Workshop Retreats.

Our emotional responses to the predicament of the self are cognitively reinforced by views, opinions, assumptions, and positions, which may be underpinned by elaborate rationales of ideological proportions originating in the collective social culture. We may have more, or less, fixed views ranging, for example, about "human nature" (as inherently aggressive, perhaps) to about oneself (maybe as "sinful" or simply "inadequate"). Through a complex range of views we interpret the world and our place in it. There are, however, several difficulties in identifying and working with views.

First, many of our views are simply absorbed from our social culture and are part of our social conditioning. They may appear to have a matter-of-fact objectivity in explaining our world, and may indeed have scientific and scholarly validity. However, what we are interested in here is the extent to which we are attached to them as supports for our sense of personal identity. For example, being a *bien pensant* liberal subjectively may reassuringly define where we stand and who we are politically, but objectively is also, arguably, an ethical and socially beneficial viewpoint.

Secondly, our views are often unexamined assumptions, lying just beyond our awareness, as in the case of much racial and gender prejudice.

Thirdly, clinging to particular views, especially if shared with others to whom we feel close, is commonly associated with conflict with those who hold opposing views, on whom we may project strong feelings which can cloud our awareness.

Donald Rothberg, in his valuable book *The Engaged Spiritual Life* (6), offers an exercise for "Developing an inventory of your views" (pp121-2), of which the following is a simplified version:

1 What are my strongest views (fixed opinions, positions, attitudes, &c.)?

2 What feelings, emotions, maybe even bodily sensations, lie beneath my expressions of these views?

3 Do I tend sometimes to exaggerate the evidence which supports those views?

4 Why is it so important for me to win the argument?

5 What might I learn from the other's views?

Heavily charged episodes and encounters can offer valuable evidence for reflection and gentle probing into the emotional needs and impulsions underlying our seemingly rational beliefs.

Adam Curle distinguished between the building up of a personal "belongingness identity" and the sense of identity obtainable by standing out and making one's mark on the world. How far we emphasise one or the other is a matter of personality and circumstance, but, either way, Curle urged us to work to replace them with an authentic "awareness identity" dependent on neither. Curle amusingly described the lifelong formation of an identity founded variously on belonging to something (or having something belong to us) and standing out from the crowd:-

> We become what we belong to and what belongs to us: our civilization, our nation, region, family, church, political party, wife and children, school, university, neighbourhood, community, house, land, books, profession, clubs and societies, social standing, investments, tastes in music and literature, views on the meaning of life and the immortality of the soul, preferences for brands of cigarettes or gin, friends, reputation, dress, eccentricities, honours, hobbies, way with the opposite sex, pictures and a thousand other things. From these we fabricate a sense of self, an identity. It is by this that we define ourselves to ourselves. It is this form of awareness we must be emptied of in order to achieve the objective awareness of the observer" — a plain awareness identity (7).

The most favoured and more or less socially licensed ways of "standing out" have not changed much since St Augustine of Hippo in the fourth century AD identified them as the acquisition of more power, prestige, wealth, and sex than the next person. Similarly, in 1984 the twentieth-century luminary, Helen Gurley Brown, editor of *Cosmopolitan* magazine, claimed that "what every woman yearns to learn" is how to have for herself "love, success, sex, money."

John Crook has updated Adam Curle's picture with the following imagined account of what might be the Buddha's impressions if he were transported to contemporary Soho:

> Gradually he would sense the profound concern his companions had for self-rewarding experiences, their

excessively ambitious workloads, their personal advertisement in conversation and their highly individualistic forms of dress and speech... Very few were concerned with personal salvation ... Most were busy enhancing material possessions and personal credentials to improve or sustain their status in the eyes of others right now in this material world of competitive buying, selling, acquiring possessions and sexual influence, all such things being markers of whom they felt themselves to be. Conversations, radio programmes, television all suggested this to be a major preoccupation of the time. Even trivial markers, the current craze for mobile phone ring tones, for example, were coming to be pointers to a young person's self-concerning individuality. He soon came to believe that behind this almost unconscious preoccupation lay a fear, a fear of being meaningless, a fear that rested upon an implicit absence of any awareness of ultimate personal value.

On the subject of mobile phones as a new support for precarious existential identity, the reclusive hero of Philip Roth's novel *Exit Ghost*, returning to New York after a long absence, remarks as follows:

For one who went frequently without talking to anyone for days at a time, I had to ask what that had previously held them up had collapsed in people to make incessant talking into a phone preferable to walking about under no one's surveillance, momentarily solitary, assimilating the streets through one's animal senses... For me it made the streets appear comic and the people ridiculous. And yet it seemed like a real tragedy, too. To eradicate the experience of separation must inevitably have a dramatic effect. What will the consequences be?

What is at issue is not necessarily a lifestyle itself, a particular pattern of behaviour, but what meaning it may give to our lives and how it may daily sustain that meaning. Two people may lead almost identical lifestyles, to all superficial appearances. For the first their lifestyle is an existential prop. The second is simply responding wholeheartedly and with active clarity to what life requires. How things are is how things are, and if they can realistically be bettered she will do her best to better them. She delights in its pleasures and weeps at the sorrows it can bring. She enjoys sex and she enjoys ice cream, because sex and ice cream can be enjoyable. She laughs but is not carried away by laughter; she weeps but is not carried away by grief.

Depending on personality we build, more or less, a fortress-like life of defensive (and aggressive) emotional habits, within a framework of self-sustaining views, reflected in the behaviour patterns of lifestyle and how we endeavour to shape our lives. It is designed to deal with a wide range of threats, all of which however originate, more, or less, in the tap root of existential "lack" — whether it be interpersonal difficulties at work, failure in intimate relationship, or chronic anxiety.

This ego fortress is most evident, physically as well as emotionally, in very neurotic and rigid personalities But it is, more generally, a self-created prison, whose "mind forged manacles" (as William Blake put it) prevent us from achieving our full potential. It recalls the story of Pinocchio, where one night the creations of the puppet master come to life and enslave their master.

The Planetary Lawsuit

Socially engaged Buddhists maintain that the restless greed and anger arising from the frustrated and fearful human condition have been socially expressed in the murderous folly of human history. Reviewing the human record of greed and general bloody-mindedness Nietzsche observed that "madness is rare in individuals, but in groups, parties, peoples, ages, it is the rule."

These emotions are embodied in society's structures, institutions and cultures, which take on a life of their own, and in turn supercharge and legitimise personal delusion as to the underlying nature of our human condition. Today the so-called "developed" world is an emotionally hungry place, insatiable in its wants and recklessly exploiting both the rest of the world and the planet itself. Acquisitiveness is institutionalised in the consumer culture and the unfettered capitalism which drives it; aggressiveness is institutionalised in a wide-ranging militarism; and existential ignorance in rancorous, sensational and inflammatory mass media.

Individuals seek refuge in a belongingness identity, in our race, our nation, our belief system or whatever, and project their fear and frustration on some other group which is seen as alien and threatening. Ideology adds a heart-warming righteousness to this reassuringly simple picture. Hence the savage warfare and the economic exploitation of the mass of human kind (and other species) by powerful and greedy minorities which make up so much of history. And hence the ease with which neighbours and workmates have killed and tortured one another in the Balkans and elsewhere on the slaughter bench of history. This is also an easy way to win elections, especially now that "terror" has been officially installed as a constant factor in public life. Such antithetical bonding extends the ancient Buddhist diagnosis of the individual condition into the social sphere. The whole story is exemplified page by page in any issue of *The Sun* or *The Daily Mirror*.

An historic, overarching lawsuit is being pursued by human civilisation against the finite reality of planet earth. It is by now clear that an economics and politics founded on seemingly endless material growth, and the consumerist lifestyle which it promotes, will soon be no longer sustainable. We shall need to manage our world on the basis of very different core values from those of the present dominant culture. This requires a bigger shift than the most radical politics; it goes to the heart of what our lives are really for. It requires an existential shift to a steady state people with steady state minds sustaining a steady state culture. Only this can maintain an ecologically sustainable economy in which quality is the only significant kind of growth.

And steady state minds are what Buddhists specialize in. Herein lies the ultimate purpose of the work we undertake to opt out of the delusive "lawsuit" in our own lives.

References

(1) *Genjo Koan.*

(2) *A Taste of Freedom* (Thailand: Bung Wai Forest Monastery, 1980, p14).

(3) *Bodhinyana*, p156.

(4) Letter to Robert Cunningham Graham.

(5) London: Windhorse, 2007.

(6) Boston: Beacon Press, 2006.

(7) *Mystics and Militants: A Study of Awareness Identity and Social Action* (London: Tavistock, 1976, p41).

Talk Two — Spiritual Materialism, Enlightenment and the Buddha Nature

Spiritual Materialism and Acquisitiveness

Chögyam Trungpa defined spiritual materialism as "a distorted, ego-centred version of spirituality; we can deceive ourselves into thinking we are developing spiritually when instead we are strengthening our egocentricity though spiritual techniques" (1). From this viewpoint, spiritual materialism is where the beginner in spiritual practice begins, and progress might be measured in terms of progressively seeing though increasingly subtle self-deceptions.

Spiritual materialism has various manifestations. For example, the precarious self may endeavour to fortify itself with righteousness by championing an absolute and literal ethical stance even in problematic situations where the rights and wrongs may be uncertain. Or, again, the nirvanic goal of spiritual endeavour may be conceived as liberation from impermanence and insubstantiality into a secure and enduring "reality". Or the spiritual goal may be seen as release from one's perceived inadequacies and imperfections into a new and perfect personality of lobotomised "enlightenment" of the kind implied by the traditional idealised images of the buddhas and bodhisattvas. Or, yet again, in terms of socially engaged Buddhism this can mean being sucked into the mentalities of secular activism which unconsciously predominate in the activist's awareness and behaviour. This makes for socially engaged Buddhists without much socially engaged Buddhism, which may be reduced to a veneer of "mindfulness" grafted onto a conventional radical activism

The spiritual materialism with which we are concerned here has to do with acquisitiveness and achievement. These mentalities, combined with individualism and competitiveness, are deeply ingrained in the modern Western psyche. The goal of enlightenment into a higher sphere of consciousness all too readily becomes the crowning ambition of the ever-hungry ego.

And so the received Buddhist training practice is translated into the familiar terms of individual mastery. A course of training is undertaken (and paid for) on retreats which transplant an Asian monasticism into a radically different culture. Here as elsewhere, instruction is provided by a qualified expert who monitors the aspirant's progress, hopefully through successively deepening insights (and corresponding promotions within the traditional hierarchy). Meditation becomes a fetishistic technology, mastery of which can lead ever upwards to the supreme goal of the enlightenment experience. Here, as in other walks of life, there is a tacit spirit of competition, of success and failure, which in some cases may deepen an already existing anxiety and sense of inadequacy. And attempts to do what good Buddhists are supposed to do can create more rigid personalities than before.

The above may be pursued as an activity extracurricular, as it were, to other parts of the aspirant's life, as a glorified hobby confined to regular periods of sitting meditation and one or more quasi-monastic retreats each year. Or, at the other extreme, it may become a cultic obsession, with household, family, employment and the lay social life all abandoned. Either scenario is sufficiently common to have attracted the term "spiritual bypassing", that is to say, a bypassing of the ups and downs of ordinary life which can provide a well grounded field of spiritual practice.

The enlightened or "awakened" state refers to opening to a higher level of consciousness, in which there is a dropping away of the previous sense of self, a falling away of craving, and a living more in the present than in the imagined future or the recreated past. However, in the first place the deluded self can only imagine enlightenment delusively, at its own present level of consciousness, and in terms of spiritual materialism as ego's ultimate acquisition. Secondly, what is supposed to be the ending of desire becomes itself an all-enveloping and obsessive desire. Thirdly, enlightenment is always just around the corner — the ultimate escape from the discomfiting present. The Tibetan teacher Gendun Rinpoche writes:

Only our searching for happiness

prevents us from seeing it.

It is like a rainbow which you run after

without ever catching it.

Although it does not exist,

it has always been there

and accompanies you every instant.

Sooner or later the aspirant may wake up to the inherent ridiculousness of the above triple irony (though others may leave, or else remain perpetually stuck, or even have insights which are nonetheless appropriated by ego — a phenomenon identified by Jung as "spiritual inflation"). In place of disappointed *belief* he or she may find sufficient *faith* — and even a kind of relief— to sustain patience, perseverance and acceptance of whatever does or doesn't come up in their practice. He or she is no longer a "spiritual failure" or "a third rate meditator" but is now able quietly to rejoice in the "suchness" of just being themselves. It was on their behalf that Master Dogen proclaimed that "every creature covers the ground its stands on, no more nor no less. It never falls short of its completeness" (2). They are released into the spirit of Alan Watts's rendering of a passage in that Chan classic, the *XinXinMing* (3):

Follow your nature and accord with the Way; saunter along and stop worrying.

When your thoughts are tied, you spoil what is genuine.

> Do not be antagonistic to the world of the senses, for when you are not it turns out to be the same as complete awakening.
>
> The wise person does not strive; the ignorant tie themselves up; if you work on your mind with your mind, how can you avoid complete confusion?

Faith in our Buddha Nature

Each of us has a True Nature, a Buddha (Awakened) Nature revealed when we become aware that mortal fear is not a necessity of the human condition. More, or less, masked in each of us, this True Nature is always there, always our potential, and always capable of manifesting itself. In each of our lives, what we do out of self-need *may* indeed be alloyed with a relatively selfless fellow spirit which partakes of our True Nature, in service and in friendship. One expression of the Buddha Nature is that everything is basically alright, something proclaimed by mystics from Mother Julian of Norwich to T.S.Eliot. Of course, the universe is also a hellish place as well. This is one of those paradoxes which you either know or you don't, and grinding away at it with logic won't help. The only way is to deploy poetry or other ways of getting in round the side, seeing things out of the corner of your eye. And beyond lies another koan "nothing matters, everything matters". This, in turn, relates to the more direct question which the great Japanese Buddhist humanist Hisamatsu Shin'ichi put to his activist followers in the wake of the Second World War: "Right now, if nothing you do is of any avail, what do you do? "

Dogen Zenji was not the first to maintain that we — and, indeed, all things — *are* the Buddha Nature (see, for example, Hui Neng's *Platform Sutra*), but his writings on it are particularly penetrating and extensive. He struggled with the question that, if practice and enlightenment are one, and we are already intrinsically enlightened, why then should we exert ourselves to practice at all? There is an analogy here with learning to play the piano or to swim; we all have the potential, but we still need to practise chords and strokes. Desire here is necessary, whereas in the realisation of our Buddha Nature it is desire itself which is the obstacle — not attainment itself, but the *desire* for attainment. Thus, in his *Zuimonki*, Dogen emphasises that "if you practice the way of the Buddha... you should expect nothing, seek nothing. Cut off the mind that seeks and do not cherish a desire to gain the fruits of Buddhahood." Similarly, in *Gyoji*, "Ceaseless Practice": "This present continuous practice is nothing other than just committing oneself to continuous practice for no other reason than to practice continuously." And, again, in *Gakudo Yojin-shu*, "Guidelines for Studying the Way", Dogen demolishes all motivations:

> "Students! Do not practice Buddha Dharma for your own sake... Do not practice Buddha Dharma to attain blissful reward. Do not practice Buddha Dharma with the thought that it might benefit others... Those who study the Way seek to be immersed in the Way. For those who are immersed in the Way all traces of enlightenment perish. Those who seek to practice the Buddha Way should first of all trust in the Buddha Way. Those who trust in the Buddha Way should trust that they are in essence within the Buddha Way, where there is no delusion, no false thinking, no confusion, no increase or decrease and no mistake. To arouse such trust and illuminate the Way in this manner, and to practice accordingly, are fundamental to studying the Way."

In short, "the realm of the Buddha is inconceivable and beyond the reach of the intellect... Only a person of great motivation can attain it. For the person who is lacking in faith it is impossible" (*Bendowa*).

Hence the eminent Dogen scholar Francis Cook maintained that

> "Dogen's Zen is the Zen of Faith, that is, a religion in which faith is the very mechanism by which the goal is achieved, and in the absence of which the door to the truth remains closed. It is therefore not simply one important element among others; it is the essential prerequisite" (4). *(How to Raise an Ox,*p22*)*.

This is so because how else can one sustain one's practice if not practising for something? Practising just for the sake of manifesting and enjoying one's Buddha Nature requires a strong faith in the existence of such a nature — and also of the inherent need to actualise it. It requires a deep faith that it is not this aspiring little self that sits on the cushion, but Buddha who sits.

I know a lot of people who have practiced Buddhism for many years and I have sangha friends going back for decades. Some of these people have never had any profound insight. They have worn out the sandal of samsara attending countless retreats. They keep coming back. They have faith. They are quiet, kindly, basically sound sort of people. What is their faith?

In some ways faith is the most mysterious of the foursome of belief, faith, insight and internalisation. Belief is a mental construct powered by the emotional need to find meaning and make sense of life. We commonly begin by reflecting on our reading of books or listening to talks about Buddhism, and deciding that what we have read or heard makes sense in the light of our experience of life. The self tends strenuously to hang on to belief and can become quite dogmatic about it. Or, if belief does not appear to be delivering its promise it may be abandoned. But sometimes when the grip on belief is relaxed there is space for faith to grow. Faith somehow intuits what is beyond belief, and in the person of faith dogmatic and proselytising fervour diminish, to be replaced with a wry smile and a shrug of the shoulders. It is simply felt to be no longer necessary to sustain one's position by argument. The person of faith who has clarity of understanding joined to a mature strength of character may have more wisdom and compassion to offer than one who has experienced striking spiritual "openings" but has not yet been able to internalise these insights into his or her life and character. Indeed, D.T. Suzuki and others have thought of faith itself as a form of *satori* in the sense of a self-forgetting.

In his "Arousing the Supreme Thought" (*Hotsu Muji Shin*) Dogen lists a great many activities which "arouse the thought of enlightenment", such as taking the refuges, bowing to the Buddha even "while you are being disturbed by demons", "practicing good to even the slightest extent possible to you", doing *zazen*, reading the sutras, making a stupa even "with a blade of grass", and so on. In short, in all these activities, however modest and limited, one formally acts as if one were Buddha — one just gets on with it. This suggests the relevance of liturgy, robes, and other traditional outward manifestations to engendering that faith which is so indispensable for Dogen Zen, and which go-getting Westerners might be inclined to dismiss as mere distractions from the great goal...

Dogen's faith appears to have much in common with the power of *punya* in the Tibetan tradition, described as follows by Rigdzin Shikpo:

> If we want to follow the Mahayana... we need to develop two kinds of accumulation. The first is the accumulation of insight, or *jnanasambhara*, through which we see the empty nature of things we cling and grasp at. The second is *punyasambhara*, the accumulation of *punya*, or power. This is a difficult word to translate. It is a somewhat mysterious strength which can accomplish many things. *Punya* is a force that can be used to change the set of our mind and

74

emotions, the way we feel about the world. *Punya* may be directed by our intention or wish. We need its power to transform our emotions, and to move the grasping, clinging mind away from self-centredness (5).

Evidently *punya* can be created by various possible aspiratory practices, ranging from doing good in the world to the actual word of Dharma which can inspire and create *punya*. Rigdzin Shikpo continues: "Having developed *punya* we then need to associate it with an intention of some kind. This is often verbalised in a kind of vow, although intention is perhaps a better way of putting it..."

Finally, at the least there is always the negative motivation that, while we see through the folly of hungering after enlightenment, yet still we suffer. It only remains either to practice in humility — and faith — or else abandon the practice altogether.

Enlightenment

The goal of enlightenment as a single stupendous, transformative, lifetime event was given undue prominence by D.T. Suzuki, the great Zen populariser of the 1960s. In fact, his perspective was only that of the Rinzai sect of Zen, which uses the great goal of enlightenment to precipitate a life-and-death kind of struggle to precipitate awakening. A more typical Buddhist view is of a personality change over a period of years, usually accompanied by insights of varying intensity. There is no doubt, however, that such existential awakening — the soteriological project — is absolutely central to Buddhism, as the path of the "Buddha" or Enlightened One.

Enlightenment is a word used with at least two different meanings. The first is that of *kensho*, a sudden and profound revelation in which "body and mind are dropped off". This can be hugely valuable in the subsequent cultivation of a wise and compassionate personality — in short an "enlightened person"(the second meaning of the word). However, we have already discussed earlier the manifold dangers of a misunderstanding and over-emphasis of enlightenment, both in distorting the whole culture of Buddhist practice and increasing the possibility of the ego-charged pseudo-spirituality of individual spiritual inflation.

In this connection, the testimony of John Crook, head of the Western Chan Fellowship may be of interest, writing out of a long experience of the problems of Western Zen practitioners:

> "We need to seek wisdom more than enlightenment and to get to know the presence of enlightenment as a basis to our lives — a form of knowing rather than short lived ecstasies. I mean that, although enlightenment experiences provide the opening insights of Dharma, few of us can attain them —- simply because the natural egotism of the average Westerner gets in the way. Such experiences cannot be attained by desire or any kind of wanting. Usually they crop up almost accidentally or when one is surprised while in a highly focussed state and the ego happens to have dropped its guard. It seems clear that one cannot train directly for such an experience. One can however train in wisdom. Meditation practices, retreat experiences, self-confrontation and encounters with teachers, the problems of life and our quest to manage ourselves all yield wisdom if one cultivates mindfulness of their meanings... Whether one can cultivate selfless kindness and compassion — that's what matters. Whether one can manage one's life wisely — that matters. Whether such understanding can be used in wise judgements in worldly affairs — that too is what matters" (6).

On several occasions Dogen made the point that "you should know that arousing practice in the midst of delusion you attain realization before you recognize it." There is a nice story about this. Someone goes out of a friend's house on a misty, rainy evening, typically British or Japanese damp weather, and wanders about rather disconsolate. Then comes back to the house, and knocks on the door. The friend lets them in. "Oh" says the friend "you are soaking wet. Look at the water all over your clothes." And the wanderer says "Oh, I didn't know." This is a nice analogy of the experience of a lifetime of practice. The changes may be quite subtle, particularly the enduring changes in our personalities. Long-term friends or partners may recognize this though may not talk about it. Dogen is referring to these subtle changes which we may not realize have taken place.

All this puts me in mind of something which Shunryu Suzuki, one of the wisest of Japanese Zen teachers who came to the West, used to say: "If you have great faith and great acceptance there is no need to worry about enlightenment. That will come along sometime as an optional extra; it doesn't matter".

----

(1) Chögyam Trungpa *Cutting through Spiritual Materialism* (Shambhala, 1973, p3).

(2) Dogen Zenji *Genjo Koan*.

(3) For the Watts and other translations, see Mu Soeng *Trust in Mind*(Wisdom, 2004).

(4) Francis Cook *How to Raise an Ox*(Wisdom, 2002, p22).

(5) Rigdzin Shikpo *Never Turn Away*(Wisdom, 2007, p132).

(6) John Crook "The Circling Birds" in *Chan Comes West* (New York: Dharma Drum Publication , 2002, pp 39-40).

Talk Three — The Practice of Emotional Awareness

1 Introduction

We return to the starting point of the first of these talks, which was Zen Master Dogen's dictum that "to study Buddhism is to study the self". "Study" here should be understood in the older sense of a deep application, a penetrating awareness. This is, however, a very ancient Dharmic practice which receives much attention in the earliest scriptures — the Pali Canon. For example, in the *Middle Length Discourses* we find the following:

> My friends, it is through the establishment of the lovely clarity of mindfulness that you can let go of grasping after past and future, overcome attachment and grief, abandon all clinging and anxiety, and awaken an unshakeable freedom of heart, here and now.

The foundation scripture here is the *Satipatthana Sutta,* designed to establish a "liberating clarity," After the calming of the mind this *Sutta* sets out a succession of awareness practices which are described as "the Four Foundations of Mindfulness" — of the body; of feelings (pleasant, unpleasant and neutral); of one's general mental state, and, finally, of the totality of one's physical and mental state. Various other classifications have been used.

It seems to me that emotional awareness is crucial, but that this needs to be practiced in the body (physical awareness). And, as explained in my First Talk, our emotional states find cognitive expression in views, opinions, beliefs and ideologies, of whose origin we also need to be aware. Also important is the awareness of impermanence — one of the three Signs of Being — and of the passing of time and the nature of our experience of time, of which Master Dogen has provided an insightful exploration. Finally there is what might be termed "environmental awareness", which seems to be the best known and most commonly practiced among Western Buddhists. This is awareness of what is happening "out there", (of which dish washing seems the oft quoted example). As to "mindfulness" and "awareness" there is at present no agreement as to definition: they are often used loosely and even interchangeably. Perhaps we should use "mindfulness" as the context in which "(bare) awareness is practised. Thus we need to be mindful in order to bring our attention to bear in awareness, as, for example, when we are struck by some misfortune or discomfiture.

Ven. Nyanaponika Thera, one of the outstanding figures in the contemporary Theravada, has observed the following, in his classic *The Heart of Buddhist Meditation*:

> Chinese Chan and Japanese Zen are the closest to the spirit of *satipatthana*. Notwithstanding the differences in method, aim and basic philosophical concepts, the connecting links with *satipatthana* are close and strong, and it is regrettable that they have hardly been noticed. In common, for instance are the direst confrontation with actuality; the merging of everyday life with the meditative life; the transcending of conceptual thought by direct observation; and the emphasis on the Here and Now.

Not least of the merits of emotional awareness practice is as an antidote to the spiritual bypassing described in my Second Talk. The Buddha's encapsulation of the Dharma as "Suffering I teach and the way out of suffering" may be unwelcome to those who have indeed taken up Buddhist practice but in their heart of hearts feel that they are already suffering enough. Mysterious and exotic orientalisms and the bright prospect of Enlightenment may seem more attractive than what can be readily dismissed as mere therapy and a watering down of the True Dharma. I am reminded of the story of the two late-night drunks searching the gutter beneath a lamp post. One of them tells a policeman who wants to know what they are up to that they are searching for a lost watch. The policeman asks the drunk why he is searching here after he has explained that the watch was in fact lost elsewhere, in a murky corner of the street. The drunk replies: "Yes, I know that, but the light is better here." Jack Kornfield, in his book *A Path with Heart*, spells it out:

> Meditation and spiritual practice can easily be used to suppress and avoid feeling or to escape from difficult areas of our lives. Our sorrows are hard to touch. Many people resist the personal and psychological roots of their suffering — there is so much pain in truly experiencing our bodies, our personal histories, our limitations ... We fear the personal and its sorrow because we have not learned how it can serve as our practice and open our hearts.

The good news is that in recent years there has been a flood of new books, by respected and established teachers, which emphasise the importance of working directly, in full awareness, with the ups and downs of our lives. Their titles include: *When Things Fall Apart; Wanting Enlightenment is a Big Mistake; The Wisdom of Imperfection; After the Ecstasy the Laundry; Everyday Zen; At Home in Muddy Water; Nothing Special Zen; Being Zen — Bringing Meditation into Life; Never Turn Away; Buddhism — Tools for Living your Life* and *Ending the Pursuit of Happiness*.

2 Three Essential Preliminaries

Before we undertake an emotional awareness practice there are three essential understandings.

First of all, it is necessary to appreciate then when we are struck by some misfortune, great or small, we need to be able to separate out the objective fact of the misfortune from how we subjectively experience it, emotionally, physically and mentally. In the *Sallatha Sutta* the Buddha explained this distinction between pain and suffering from pain as follows:

> When afflicted with a feeling of pain those who lack inner awareness sorrow, grieve and lament, beating their breasts and becoming distraught. So they feel two pains, physical and mental. It is just like being shot with an arrow, and right afterwards being shot with a second one, so that they feel two arrows.

It is common experience that individuals tend to respond in often quite different ways when all are struck by a common affliction, as with patients in the same hospital ward and with much the same medical condition. Thus, when we receive that letter of dismissal, or news of that feared diagnosis, it were best to resist the impulse to respond immediately and instead to open in meditative awareness to how it *feels*. We shall then be in a better position to respond without our judgement being so clouded by fear, panic, anger and similar emotional *responses*.

In the second place, it is important to understand the difference between pain, whether physical or emotional, on the one hand, and our characteristic response, which is called *dukkha*, in Pali, and rather misleadingly translated as "suffering". Here it will be helpful to go back briefly to basics, to the Three Signs of Being — insubstantitiality, impermanence and *dukkha* (suffering). Because of the first two, suffering arises. They engender in us a sense of *lack*, a profound existential insecurity. We struggle to evade this by attempting to fill our lives with behaviours and ideas which we hope will give us a strong sense if identity, and, conversely, by striving to evade all those misfortunes, discomfitures and set-backs which undermine our sense of being a Somebody who has control over his or her life. Our characteristic responses are summarised in the traditional

Three Fires of anger (and, socially, militarism), greed (and consumerism), and ignorance (the mass media).

Thus, suffering, in the Buddhist sense, can be characterised as the emotional pain arising from the futility of our attempts to evade whatever threatens our delusive sense of identity. Such evasions may take the form of strongly held beliefs, such as that the spiritual ideal is to be able to face physical or emotional pain fearlessly. This attempts to fortify an impregnable identity of "fearlessness". Yet the more we struggle to deny or somehow rid ourselves of fear, the more frightened we become. Ultimately our only liberation lies in the wholehearted acceptance of fear, breathing awareness into the heart of the pain, feeling its texture, becoming intimate with it. Thus, in the *Udana* the oldest scripture in the Pali Canon, the Buddha advises on what's to be done with a leaking roof — take it right off, and then the rain can no longer fall through it...

Our evasions in the face of life's discomfitures have strong emotional roots, of which we tend to be unaware. Some of our evasions are hot ones, most notably anger, particularly if it is felt as righteous, reasonable (and maybe even well-researched!) anger. This takes our mind off the sense of frustration and powerlessness which causes our suffering and gives the ego the boost it craves. This works even better if we can project it onto someone else or some other group whom, we believe, can be held responsible. "*Someone* must be to blame!" Then there are the "I am to blame" evasions, notably self-pity and guilt. Here we unconsciously feel we can mitigate our suffering somehow by beating *ourselves* up. These are evasions where we are so over-indulgent with the feelings that we act them out without fully experiencing them. Then there are the "cooler" evasions, of which four are noteworthy: denial, escaping into busyness, objectification and rationalisation, where we try to bury the feeling with thinking. These are commonly found working together. We try to bury our emotional response, to view the misfortune as somehow external to us, to strive for a "rational" solution, and to immerse ourselves being busy working at it. This is one way, for example, of evading the emotional pain of an alarming medical diagnosis. In my experience these four are common masculine responses, sometimes accompanied by an inability to describe what is actually being felt. Most of us seem to have one or two favourite evasions, and it would be worthwhile to reflect what these might be. However, the basic emotional awareness practice is simply to become intimate with just how it feels, which itself can expose and dissolve whatever evasions are overlaying the raw emotions.

Thirdly, in undertaking emotional awareness practice it is important to develop mindfulness of our habitual response to the many and various discomfitures encountered in life, ranging from the loss of some favourite trinket to the prospective loss of our lives. What is required is to replace the above evasive responses with a spirit of positive and curious enquiry, neither suppressing the response nor expressing it. Of course, it takes considerable practice to reverse our customary and deeply embedded reaction to bad news. Thus the Zen philosopher Hubert Benoit warns as follows:

> If an humiliating circumstance turns up, offering me a marvellous chance of initiation, at once my imagination strives to conjure up what appears to me to be in danger... It does everything to restore me to that habitual state of satisfied arrogance in which I find a transitory respite, but also the certainty of further distress. In short, I constantly defend myself against that which offers to save me; foot by foot I fight to defend the very source of my unhappiness.

This practice appears to receive some treatment in all the Buddhist traditions, but especially in the Tibetan, where beginning students are exhorted to make the difficulties in their lives into their path of practice. "Grant that I may be given appropriate difficulties and sufferings on this journey so that my heart may be truly awakened" is a prayer they recite. Similar teachings are to be found in other inner-path religious traditions. This by the Persian Sufi poet Rumi (version by Coleman Barks) is particularly eloquent:

> This being human is a guest house.
>
> Every morning a new arrival.
>
> A joy, a depression, a meanness,
>
> some momentary awareness comes
>
> as an unexpected visitor.
>
> Welcome and entertain them all
>
> even if they're a crowd of sorrows,
>
> who violently sweep your house
>
> empty of its furniture.
>
> Still treat each guest honourably
>
> he may be clearing you out
>
> for a new delight.
>
> The dark thought, the shame, the malice,
>
> meet them at the door laughing,
>
> and invite them in.
>
> Be grateful for whoever comes,

for each has been sent

as a guide from beyond.

Indeed, there is a universal wisdom here, as in Shakespeare's *As You Like It*: "Sweet are the uses of adversity which, like the toad, ugly and venomous, yet wears a precious jewel in his head."

3 Where Does Your Shoe Pinch?

The ups and downs of our lives constitute our inner workshop — from despair to elation, the whole gamut of pains and pleasures. Yes, pleasure too, is worth opening up to the light of bare awareness. Is it a pleasure that burns with the smoke of evasion — the need for the lonely, vulnerable ego to maximise the red letter days? Or does it burn with the bright flame of the "sheer pleasure" of an unconditional awareness? With practice we can begin to sense which is which at least at the more extreme ends of the continuum.

Working with our suffering, however, concentrates and motivates best, and especially where the pain is acute. The value of this practice is well expressed by Zen Master Susan Murphy, in *Upside Down Zen*:

> What is the sharpest fact in your life right now? Take a moment to consider your most haunting terror, your most persistent aggravation or relentless criticism of yourself, or a deep pain you have taken upon yourself. Feel it in your body. That terror, aggravation, shame or sadness is your dearest enemy ... all your creative power for the Way is to be found right there ... so turning that way is turning toward your true freedom ... Such is the blessing to be found in a curse. Practice is not just a matter of breaking through the fact of suffering, but realising that suffering *is* a Dharma gate which lies open to you.

85

So a first task is to take stock of our lives, and to identify what discomfits us, great and small. And how we typically respond to it. This, in itself, is a useful undertaking. If Buddhism is essentially about "suffering and the way out of suffering", then how about you? Most of us, for example, experience some deep sense of inadequacy, or maybe guilt. At a deeper level still we may feel that something is profoundly lacking in our lives, or we may be haunted by existential fear or anxiety. Or we may suffer the physical pain arising from ill health or disability. At the other extreme we may be dogged by some comparatively petty annoyance, like the untidiness of a shared household. And then there are all the difficulties and discomfitures that are commonly encountered at work and in families and relationships. And here is Diana Winston, of the (American) Buddhist Peace Fellowship on the pain of disempowerment and despair at the prospects for our planet:

> I have been much struck by my own (and others') painful sense of hopelessness and disempowerment in the face of the deteriorating global situation. It doesn't matter that I have been an activist for twenty years. It doesn't make any difference the fact that in the last few months I've been to rallies, painted placards, and lobbied. At the bottom of it all there's this horrible feeling that it's all kind of hopeless.

The taste of liberation is one taste, and so insight arising from working with a comparatively minor aggravation can nonetheless be beneficial when we are struck by some greater misfortune. However, great grief has the potential for great insight, so it were best to work with the strongest emotions that we can handle.

4 The Practice of Emotional Awareness

Chögyam Trungpa summarised the practice as follows: "Let yourself be in the emotion. Go through it, give in to it,experience it... then the most powerful energies become absolutely workable rather than taking you over, because there is nothing to take over if you are not putting up any resistance." This is amplified by Morrie Schwartz, as quoted by Jack Kornfield in his book *After the Ecstasy, the Laundry:*

> Take any emotion — love for a woman, or grief for a loved one, or what I'm going through — fear and pain from a deadly illness. If you hold back from the emotions — if you don't allow yourself to go all the way through them — you can never get to be detached, you're too busy being afraid. You're afraid of the pain, you're afraid of the grief. You're afraid of the vulnerability that loving entails. But by throwing yourself into these emotions ... you experience them fully and completely. You know what pain is. You know what love is. You know what grief is. And only then can you say, "Alright, I've experienced that emotion... now I'm free to detach from that emotion..."

On the face of it, it's easy enough to understand. Suffering arises from our ultimately hopeless struggle to evade physical and emotional pain. If we can accept that pain in the depths of our heart, then we are released from suffering. However, the impulse to try to evade pain is perhaps the deepest instinct that we have. Hence the practice of emotional awareness — of becoming intimate with pain — is a demanding and lifetime undertaking, to be pursued on a strong meditative foundation.

This practice is to be pursued on and off the cushion, using whatever devices prove helpful. For example, in some cases it may be helpful to recall and re-imagine episodes in which the pain was particularly acute and vivid, as in the case of an interpersonal encounter. Others may find it helpful endlessly to repeat a question like "What does it *feel* like?" until it envelopes their life. But one thing for sure is that this is a practice which requires to be pursued as much as possible in the body; as Master Dogen observed, "Awareness of the body is the body's awareness." Ezra Bayda, in his book *Being Zen*, explains:

> Intense emotional distress can leave us feeling lost and overwhelmed. In these darkest moments the practice is to bring awareness to the centre of the chest, breathing the painful emotions, via the inbreath, directly into the heartspace. It's as if we were breathing the swirling physical sensations right into the heart. Then, on the outbreath, we simply exhale. We're not trying to do or change anything; we're simply allowing our heart centre to become a wider container of awareness within which to experience distress.

All our emotional experiences are at the same time physical experiences, as in the well-known sensations of fear or anger, and it with these that we must endeavour to become intimate. With practice we may even become aware of the colour, taste and smell of some acute emotional pain — as with the crimson of anger, or the blue of self-pity.

Three personal testimonies may provide useful pointers. They are taken from several such in Susan Moon's valuable book *Not Turning Away: The Practice of Engaged Buddhism*. The first I have chosen is a response to the distress caused by racism: "Buddhism allows me to be right were I am at this moment. I do not have to condemn or approve my anger and pain. Neither do I have to deny those feelings. I can simply be with them, observing their rising and falling, their impact on me and others." The second is about childhood abuse by a father: "If shame is all you have, embrace what you have. Honour it and care for it with all your attention and kindness. In your own grief you will find the power to convert shame into compassion." Thirdly, the heartfelt and absolute embracing of chronic mental illness: "For me, recovering from mental illness would be like recovering from being human. The manic highs and depressive lows I have experienced for all these years are, for better or worse, part of who I am."

5 Emotional Awareness as a Liberative Path

How does this practice of a deepening intimacy with our discomfitures and distress open us up to a liberative acceptance and, indeed, a veritable empowerment? The question is of more than mere speculative interest, and understanding can provide valuable support and encouragement to the practice.

Krishnamurti once held up his thumb and forefinger and declared that all the miseries of the world arise from that little gap, the difference between this (which is desired) and that (which is rejected). He is referring to that constant flicker between desire and rejection which is one of the first phenomena we notice when we sit in meditation with a sufficiently still mind as to be able to observe the root activity of the mind. This is sometimes called The Higher Third. This mode of experience when we are able to rest in the *suchness* of a situation, just-how-it-is, brings an immediate sense of release from the constant struggle for this and against that which puts lines on our face and stresses, tightens and wears out the whole of our body. At last we begin to sense our "true nature", our "Buddha Nature" where suffering loses its grip.

This suchness has been expressed in Zen through koans, poetry and ways of pointing beyond the logic of this and that, to just-how-it-is. It is found, for example, in both contemporary Western haiku and ancient Japanese *waka*, as in these examples from an Irish haiku poet, Jim Norton, and the celebrated Japanese 13th Century master, Eihei Dogen (where it takes the form of a veritable koan):

Coughing   If you ask "What is Buddha?"

and the stranger upstairs   an icicle

coughs too   hanging from a mosquito net

The latter recalls a koan which asks the student where there is a place which, in winter, is neither hot nor cold. In the experience of suchness, that is a place where the temperature is just as it is, beyond the relativities of "hot" and "cold". Dogen again, in his *Eihei Koroku*, writes: "Do you not see, the clouds in the highest mountains disperse themselves — what 'far' or 'near' is there? The river winds its way though the valley without THIS or THAT." As the ancient Chan poem, the *XinXinMing*, reminds us, "When you are not attached to anything, all things are as they are."

So, whether it is a difficult colleague at work, a spouse behaving disagreeably, an obstreperous child, or a burdensome aged parent, in Dogen's words, "every creature covers the ground it stands on; it never falls short of its completeness." Quite suddenly we may, for the very first time, see any of these troublous people in their own light, not ours, and the relationship can become more manageable

The power of suchness can also liberate us from the suffering of impermanence, with help from koans like the magnificent "There is no time, what is memory?" The Buddha said: "It is a way of deep meditation to see that the past no longer exists and the future has not yet come, and to dwell at ease in the present moment, free from desire. When a person lives in this way they give up all anxiety and regrets, letting go of all binding desires and cutting the fetters that prevent them being free."

At times when we may feel lonely, afraid and unable to find any meaning in our lives, if we open whole heartedly to our despair we can find ourselves experiencing that creatively rich suchness that has about it a bitter authenticity. This is what Keats called negative capability, "when a man is capable of being in uncertainties, mysteries, doubts, without any irritable reaching after fact and reason."

A valuable first hand testimony to the workings of emotional awareness comes from Darlene Cohen, in her book *Turning Suffering Inside Out*. Cohen is a Zen teacher and a massage therapist who has for long suffered from severe and progressively crippling arthritis. She writes as follows:

> People sometimes ask me where my healing energy comes from. How, in the midst of this pain, this implacable slow crippling, can I encourage myself and other people? My answer is that my healing comes from my bitterness itself, my despair, my terror ... I dip down into that muck again and again, and then am flooded with its healing energy. Despite the renewal and vitality I get from facing my deepest fears, I don't go willingly when they call. I've been around that wheel a million times: first, I feel the despair, but I deny it for a few days; then, its tugs become more insistent in proportion to my resistance: finally, it overwhelms me and pulls me down, kicking and screaming all the way. It's clear I am caught, so at last I give up to this reunion with the dark aspect of my adjustment to pain and loss. Immediately the release begins: first, peace, and then the flood of vitality and healing energy.

> I can never simply give up to my despair when I first feel it stir. You'd think after a million times with a happy ending, I could give up right away and just say, "Take me, I'm yours" but I never can. I always resist ... It's staring defeat and annihilation in the face that's so terrifying; I must resist until it overwhelms me. But I've come to trust it deeply. It's enriched my life, informed my work, and taught me not to fear the dark.

6 Clarity and joy, self-love and playfulness

When we begin to sense that our lifelong and unwinnable law suit with reality is simply *unnecessary* we experience a liberative relief, a clarity and joy, and a release into a strange playfulness in the midst of the world's black tragi-comedy. Released into a limitless, flowing world of great beauty and infinite possibilities, we dance the dance of impermanence and insubstantiality. For, as Oscar Wilde observed, that world "is in too much of a mess to be taken seriously." Which is why it is said of the bodhisattvas that they go down to rescue souls out of hell and treat it as if it were a fairground.

Self-acceptance frees off self love, of just who we are, beyond better or worse. And to love ourselves is surely the most difficult kind of love. For a start, is there not a danger of falling into narcissism or self-righteousness? I think not, if self love awakens with the objective clarity of authentic insight, as something given, not taken. But it may be asked how can I love a self which has been guilty of so many follies which have hurt others? Unless we "honour" our follies we remain divided against ourselves. But to honour them is not to condone them or forget and dismiss them. Rather is it to remain in awareness of them as hurts we have committed against others and ourselves, accepted with compassion for ourselves. Thus, in the Soto Zen tradition at the dawn meditation the Verse of Atonement is chanted: "All evil karma ever committed by me since of old, on account of my beginningless greed, anger and ignorance, born of my body, mouth and thought, now I atone for it all."

Self love, springing from wholehearted acceptance of ourselves, is made possible by faith — faith in our Buddha Nature, our basic goodness. The dawning of faith is the major waymark on the Way of emotional awareness, sustained previously only by belief. It is the faith of Mother Julian of Norwich, and of mystics down to the poet T. S. Eliot: "All shall be well, and all manner of thing shall be well." "All manner of things" and not only the self. Yet it is authentic self love which makes possible unreserved love for everything else. As the Buddha observes in the *Udana*: "I visited all quarters with my mind, but did not find any dearer than myself. His or her self is likewise dear to every other, and those who love themselves will never harm another."

7 Active Compassion: Opening to the Bodhisattva Path

Dwelling in suchness we are relieved of our self-centred preoccupation, our root priority of sustaining a strong self-identity. We are released into an open awareness-identity, in which the dualism of self and other begins to dissolve into the experience of unity consciousness, of at-oneness with all that was formerly sensed as other.

Arguably, it seems at this stage there is possibly some flaw, some incompletion, by which the adept can get stuck in a blissful state of quietism. Could it be that this is the loftiest and most subtle form of spiritual materialism? In our own time proponents of a socially engaged Buddhism have been reproached for failing first to gain "enlightenment", lest their spiritual immaturity should only contribute to the existing confusion in the world. Unfortunately, for contemporary Westerners, at any rate, "enlightenment" tends to be a rather exclusive and remote experience, especially if the term refers not just to a momentary experience but to the substantially completed cultivation of an enlightened personality, that is, of wisdom and compassion. Hence this view was dubbed "Mañana Buddhism" by that doughty champion of engaged Buddhism, David Brandon. And at that time, another such, Roshi Robert Aitken maintained that it is through skilful awareness in navigating the ups and downs of social activism that we can ripen the wisdom and compassion of the bodhisattva. Master Dogen, the greatest of Zen philosopher monks, made it clear that "those who regard worldly affairs as

93

an obstacle to their training do not realize that there is nothing such as worldly affairs to be distinguished from the Way." Dogen scholar Hee-Jin-Kim has argued the importance of *daitoku*, of making an active project of our lives. In Dogen's view things, events, relations were not just given, but were possibilities, projects and tasks that can be carried out and understood as self-expressions and self-activities of the Buddha Nature. This did not imply a complacent acceptance of a given situation, but requires our strenuous efforts to transform and transfigure it. This element of transformation has been grossly neglected by Dogen scholars."

The other side of the suchness coin is the world experienced as this-*versus*-that, (or, more accurately, the experience of suchness turns it into this-*and*-that). In this world as we age, death does indeed come closer; we still have too little time to write the report required by our boss; we are faced with choices about the resolution of a difficult personal relationship; we may lose our job and have to clarify options as our next step. Sometimes we may experience such situations with the eye of a newfound suchness, and at other times in terms of this-and-that. This has been called a "salt-and-pepper" stage. But as we embody our wisdom this seeming paradox (to the logical mind) dissolves into a single, unified experience. As the *Heart Sutra* says, "Form is no other than emptiness, emptiness no other than form." The following paraphrase of a teaching by R.H. Blyth points to this "one mind":

> Things may be hopeless,
>
>> but not dispiriting;
>
> Unjust,
>
>> but not hateful;
>
> Beautiful,
>
>> but not desirable;

Loathsome,

but not rejected.

Or, as Donald Rothberg has it: "Righteous indignation with a smile, and deep inner pain without bitterness or revenge."

It is through years of maturing and creative awareness of the suffering in our lives and in others' that we grow into wisdom and compassion, into a self at ease which is an unburdened self which cannot but be open to the needs of others. As William Blake put it, our windows of perception are cleansed, and this clarity enables us to move in the world without the "mind forged manacles" of fear and ideology.

At the extreme end of emotional awareness practice is the "Dark Night" when the hero or heroine hits rock bottom, in total despair, with nowhere else to go. What may happen then may be intuitive, spontaneous, and unprepared by any overt spiritual practice. It is a revelatory "acceptance" that frees us of all illusions, all evasions, whether of activism or quietism, and which enables authentic and appropriate response to what the situation may require. There is considerable biographical testimony for such "despair and empowerment". In Easterhouse, a huge squalid housing estate on the outskirts of Glasgow, Cathy McCormack, spoke of her despair after seven years of unemployment and crushing adversity: "I was so broken by it that I felt there was no point in living. I wanted to go to sleep and never wake up again. Then one day something happened. It was a kind of awakening; almost a spiritual experience... I understood that my life is here in this place, and no fantasy of escape would help. This is where the wains must grow up and make their lives; here we must survive or perish together" (Reported by Jeremy Seabrook, in the *Myth of the Market*). Cathy McCormack was enabled to empower her fellow tenants, and to initiate regeneration projects to reverse the cycle of despair and deprivation.

The above exemplifies the archetype of "the broken hearted (and hence open hearted) warrior" — the bodhisattva, — described by John Welwood:

> If we are to remain open to life and engage with our world rather than succumbing to depression or cynicism we must learn how to live with a broken heart. The heart cannot actually *break* — it can only *break open*. When we feel both love for this work and the pain of this world of ours, together, at the same time, the heart *breaks out* of this shell. Then we feel the world inside us and not separated from us. To live with a broken heart is to live life at full strength.
>
> When the heart breaks open, it marks the beginning of a real love affair with this world. It is a broken hearted love affair, without the conventional hope and expectation. Only with this fearless love can we be of real help to ourselves or anyone else in this difficult age. *The broken hearted warrior is an essential archetype for our time.*

Here the gateless gate opens to the great koan NOTHING MATTERS, EVERYTHING MATTERS. Or, as Gary Snyder, poet and activist, puts it, "Knowing that nothing needs to be done is where we move from." We have to act as if our heads were on fire and the situation urgent, and yet as if we had all the time in the world.

Talk Four — Varieties of Spiritual Materialism

1 - A Buddhist heaven?

Spiritual materialism is a perception of spiritual phenomena arising from a delusive and egocentric mind state, which appropriates and falsifies ideas of spirituality the better to fill its sense of existential *lack*. Spiritual materialism is therefore where we practitioners start from, some more and some less, depending what kind of genetic and karmic hand we were dealt at birth and by our upbringing. It is important for us to beware of the typical delusions encountered on our spiritual journey if we are not to lose our way. Many have done so, including a few who reached positions of some spiritual eminence.

In Talk Two in this series I drew attention to the distortions arising from acquisitiveness and achievement in pursuit of the much prized goal of "enlightenment". Here I shall introduce four other varieties of spiritual materialism.

Faced with a deepening awareness of the impermanence and insubstantiality of what passes as "reality", and of the futility of the struggle to fill our sense of lack in the more gross and obvious ways, the self tends to cling to more subtle assumptions that hover on the edge of awareness. Surely there must be *something* to provide *the* support? It might be "Buddhism", "the Dharma", the hope of "Enlightenment", or maybe just an undefined "something". For many years, following D.T. Suzuki, I assumed there was some "authentic" reality out there temporarily obscured and distorted by my delusion.

Behind these anxieties of the individual practitioner lies the ancient and widespread belief in an underlying, eternal, transcendental unity called God, the Tao, the Absolute. In more sophisticated Dharma, this becomes the reification and solidification of emptiness, into something more real and reliable than the world of manifest reality, of form. This apparently dominant view in Japanese Buddhism provoked the Critical Buddhism of the nineties, which argued that seeing the mundane in terms of the absolute diminishes distinctions and values. This defines that, good defines bad, and ethical values are disembedded. At worst such a perspective can become an accessory to social injustice, as in the case of Japanese "Imperial Way Zen". Unfortunately the rejection of this metaphysical caricature of emptiness led some of the Critical Buddhists to reject emptiness itself as opportunistic mystification.

There is a memorable passage in Dogen's *Genjo Koan* arguing the absence of any ultimate reality beyond our shared, variegated and fragile experience. He observes that when we are in a boat and out of sight of land, for us there is only a circle of ocean, and that for us *is* how it is. Yet for a fish or a bird it is experienced very differently. Arising from their impermanence and insubstantiality phenomena are infinitely variable and contingent. And, as Wittgenstein reminds us in our own day, indefinables like "self", "time", and "death" have no substantive existence, but nonetheless we can recognise and discuss them. As bodhisattvas we become at home and at one in the impermanence and insubstantiality of all phenomena and not least of ourselves. It is this that releases us into the playfulness of life, so it is said that bodhisattvas can go down into hell as if it were a fair ground. Released from the structured solidifications which conventionally fortify our selfhood, we are opened to infinite possibilities. As Oscar Wilde observed, our world is in too serious a state to be taken seriously. In Zen, the people of faith are the people of play. The Japanese call this lightness karumi and it is much valued in their art and literature. However, as the underlying sadness of clowns reminds us, this is not the whole story.

Akin to the spiritual materialism which solidifies emptiness is a no less escapist version for which the world of form is no more than *maya* — illusion, a passing dream. This, also, devalues humanity, its sufferings, and its values, as no more than a passing show. Socially engaged Buddhists are all too familiar with such nihilistic proponents of "emptiness".

The Chan and Zen masters anticipated this tendency to cling to emptiness. Thus Sengcan, in his celebrated poem *On Trust in the Heart*, warned: "If you get rid of phenomena, then everything is lost. If you follow after the Void you turn your back on the very substance of things." And the world emptied of self-construction does indeed have a vivid *suchness* a *thusness*, a pungent reality which contrasts with the pale, devitalised world which reflects our root existential fear. The fifteenth-century Zen master Ikkyu exclaimed

> If your eyes see
>
> And your ears hear
>
> Not a doubt will you cherish —
>
> And how naturally the rain drops
>
> From the eaves!

Thus, instead of clinging to emptiness we embrace the paradox proclaimed in the *Heart Sutra* that "form is no other than emptiness, emptiness no other than form." As the old song has it "Row, row, row the boat, gently down the stream, verily, verily, verily, verily life is just a dream." It is indeed, but rowing is hard work; it raises blisters on our hands. The Zen master bangs his stick on the floor, and we return to our stricken planet. As haiku master Issa reminds us: "We walk on the roof of hell and view the flowers". And so, *emptied* of self - need, in wholehearted acceptance, and liberated from our long law suit with reality, we pass through the gateless gate and we get to work.. As Gary Snyder reminds us: "Knowing that nothing needs to be done is where we start from." Nothing matters, everything matters.

2 - Peace, perfect peace

Of the versions of the Blessed Other (above) peace, a peaceful mind, is particularly longed for. As the Zen saying has it, "for we who are fleas on the hot griddle of life, the fleas that jump must fall, and the fleas that fall must jump." The struggle to sustain an adequate self can be a wearying busyness. For many outsiders, this is what Buddhism is all about — the tranquil Buddha *rupa*, the still figure on the meditation cushion.

There is no question about the need to still the busy mind so that its surface becomes less ruffled and agitated, and we can observe the monsters that breed at lower depths. Some contemplative detachment from the feelings and thoughts which customarily drive us is essential. Hence the practice of *samatha*, stilling the mind, is, in one form or another, essential to all meditation traditions. The other aspect of meditation is *vipassana*, looking deeply into the still mind, whether posing a question, or simply in bright and active awareness. Some of us are better at one, some at the other, but we all need at least a bit of both. Unfortunately, it seems that, for many, *samatha*, stilling the mind, is as far as it goes. A meditation retreat is for them a kind of therapy, a merciful, though temporary, relief from the turmoil, conflict and busyness of their working week. It is certainly not seen as an opportunity to confront and befriend their personal demons, to which they may not even so far have managed an introduction. "My mind was in turmoil ... I just couldn't sit *properly*." On the contrary, when the shit hits the fan, and the defences are temporarily breached, is the best time to sit. It's prime time for that emotional awareness which can spin straw into gold. A well-rooted calmness and imperturbability of mind cannot be willed. But gradually it can be nurtured through the practice of bare emotional awareness.

3 - "Becoming a Buddha" — the idealised self

Many are drawn to Buddhism — and quite properly — by the image of the Buddha: good, peaceful, wise, and, in a word, perfect. The hungry self longs to be like that, for here, as elsewhere, the start of the Great Way lies in a spiritual materialism. There is no better filler of lack than righteousness and the invincibility of perfection. We badly want to be like that, we want our spiritual guides and exemplars to be like that, and we want others to be like that (and especially when they appear to threaten us in some way). And so, we resort to the only ready tool which appears to be available — the exercise of the will. There are plenty of *paramitas* to perfect. As a consequence we can become dismayingly priggish and patronising These self-conscious role players are not difficult to spot. They try too hard. They don't ring true, much like a counterfeit coin. Probably they fear that if they allow themselves to become intimate with their underlying feelings and desires then self-indulgence and a host of vices will flood forth. Spiritual practice is equated with quietism and self-effacement and desiccation of the passions is seen as a virtue.

The will is valuable for ethical emergency stops "Just don't do it!". But it cannot alone press into shape a moral personality of character and integrity. Its real job is to sustain those spiritual practices which, over time, can ripen a moral *personality*. Where we are faced with some difficult moral dilemma, where what needs to be done goes slap against our emotional imperatives, this ripening may take patience and time (if time there is). Ripeness is all.

In all this I sense some difference in emphasis between different Buddhist teachers and traditions. For example, on the one hand there is the exercise of the will in beaming loving kindness towards our enemies (or ourselves). Some seem to find this comes readily enough; others sense some resistance and inauthenticity. Some teachers evidently have reservations about this time-hallowed practice (perhaps those, like Mark Epstein, with a psychotherapeutic background). Arguably it smacks too much of behavioural conditioning. For my part, and at least as a preliminary, I would prefer first to turn the search within. Our feeling of enmity is *our* problem, and not that of the other towards whom we feel it. When we expose it to a well practiced bare awareness it softens, changes character, becomes less self-obsessed. And it is then that we may be better placed to experience the other more positively. (There are interesting echoes here between different wider spiritual practice traditions, like *via negativa* contrasted with *via positiva*).

In Zen, and, indeed, in Japanese culture, there are warnings about the delusive nature of our longing for perfection, whether in ourselves or elsewhere. Thus there is the saying that "the Buddha is still practising with us". The authenticity of the Zen bowl on my mantelpiece is marked by an imperfection, which I am told was made deliberately by the potter as a finishing touch. The beautiful heroine in a Nō play always has a hair deliberately out of place. If there were perfection there could be no suchness. If there were no suchness there could be no liberation from the tyranny of longing for this as against that, in a word, for perfection.

If we are attached to some "spiritual" ideal about what a Buddhist teacher should be like this is to confuse the inevitable differences in personality and temperament with spiritual maturity. Some are cheerful and easy going, others cantankerous and demanding. Some are passionate and excitable, others are slow and mindful. And so on, in endless variety. Indeed, one result of being free of the struggle to become a secure, well-defended and generally accepted self and, instead, just being open to our emotions and who we really are, is that we become more utterly ourselves and hence more unique than ever. Jack Kornfield has remarked on what an eccentric lot are Buddhist teachers. And Ram Dass observed that years of spiritual discipline had left his quirky personality intact but had enabled him to become "a connoisseur of my neuroses." It is thus hardly surprising that Buddhist teachers are such a variegated and eccentric lot.

A different — or just a more extreme — case is where an excellent teacher fails, in his or her conduct, to live up to their teachings. There are numerous instances of effective teachers who fail to teach by example. These doubtless include worthies in the history of Buddhism whose biographies have been long ago cleaned up and made more presentable. In such cases it is possible to speculate endlessly why it was they ran off the rails. When I first encountered this as a student I wondered whether I should quit an otherwise helpful teacher. Eventually I stayed. And I have never forgotten my self-centred moralising, the absence of an open-hearted compassion, and my futile anxiety to find a satisfying explanation and do "the right thing."

It should be added that the idealisation of teachers has sometimes led to their community turning a blind eye for too long to abuses to do with sex, power and money.

4 Buddhist fundamentalism

The essence of spiritual materialism lies in the delusive struggle of the self to sustain a secure identity by clinging to ideas and behaviours which are believed to possess a spiritual validation. This is particularly evident in the field of ethics and morality.

The sense of inadequacy experienced by many gives rise to a clinging to being GOOD and RIGHT as a self-centred affirmation rather than a compassionate response to the demands of a situation or problem "out there". Thus, arguments are commonly less about the merits of this or that position in a dispute and more about being in the right oneself and demonstrating how wrong one's adversary is — and the more black and white the better. Fortunes have been squandered in legal process to secure the right to ownership of some trifling bit of garden along a disputed boundary. But this is as nothing when set against the opposing "wars against evil" of the twenty-first century.

Faced with the uncertainty and complexity of many ethical problems and situations there are Buddhists whose need for righteousness makes a dogma out of the ethical precepts. These literalists treat Buddhism as if it were a "religion of the book", where the precepts must be applied literally no matter what the circumstances. There is a strong attachment here to "the letter of the law," seemingly arising from a desire for absolute moral certainty. Yet even when trying to keep one precept we may violate another, as, for example, if we were to lie in order to save a life ("No, there's no one hiding here!"). Moreover a great many situations arise in public and private life which are sufficiently complex as to put us in some moral perplexity. Abortion, medically assisted suicide for the terminally ill, and armed peacekeeping are examples which have attracted some controversy in Buddhist circles.

As opposed to the literalist (or scriptural fundamentalist), for the situationist the ethical precepts are the valued *starting point* for an investigation requiring meditative clarity, freedom from the itch to be absolutely certain, and the courage to risk making what may turn out to be the wrong decision. We can only act out of our compassion for all involved (including ourselves) and do our honest best.

The majority of Western Buddhists appear to be situationists, but there are prominent Asians also, and not least the Dalai Lama. For example, the second issue of *Raft* (Winter 1989/90) was devoted to a wide ranging symposium on euthanasia, designed to represent a spectrum of opinion. In fact, of the five prominent Buddhist teachers who contributed four assumed the situationist position. One of these, Ajahn Sumedho, wrote as follows:

> We seem to want to take absolute, moral and fixed positions on such questions as "How do you feel about euthanasia?" Our minds tend to be conditioned to take a fixed view on [such] issues, and we interpret life morally. But the Buddha-mind is not fixed on a position and is able to take into account all the things that are affecting a given situation. This means that sometimes it seems a bit wishy-washy and we would like Buddhism to come through with a strong moral position; and yet what Buddhism has to offer is not moral positioning but real morality; the opportunity to take responsibility for your own decisions.

This is not some quandary of contemporary Western Buddhism. In all the Buddhist traditions examples can be found of situational morality. The great 13th century Zen master Dogen, for example, observed that "Good and evil arise with circumstances ... What is good and what is bad are difficult to determine ... Good is understood differently in different worlds" (Hee-Jin Kim, *Eihei Dogen: Mystical Realist*, Wisdom, 2004, pp221–223). The present state of the world offers many examples. Anarchic states are increasingly common, with much random butchery of the helpless by drug crazed soldiery or ideologically crazed fundamentalists. Such situations require multi-skilled peacemaking teams of mediators, aid workers and others. These must of necessity include specially trained soldiers able to make a judicious use of force where it is clearly essential to protect the innocent and enable more peaceful remedies to be applied. For some Buddhist situationists even the Christian definition of the Just War may be helpful. These are perennial problems, going back to the Buddha's time. In the *Cakkavatti Sihanada Sutta* of the

Digha Nikaya he is said to have justified the existence of military force for the purpose of protection as long as it is done "according to *dhamma*".

Talk Five — The Zen of Intimate Relationship

Context and Preliminaries

Every sector and phase of our lives is potentially valuable as a field of Buddhist practice, whether it be work, parenting, intimate relationship, ageing, loss and bereavement, and so on. In all these fields we commonly experience some more or less painful dissatisfaction. This we attempt to resolve within that field unaware of its deeper origin in our characteristic existential sense of *lack*. Thus Erich Fromm remarked as follows of the majority of patients he observed in therapy:

> They complain of being depressed, of having insomnia, being unhappy in their marriages, not enjoying their work, and any number of similar troubles. They usually believe that this or that particular symptom is their problem, and if only they could get rid of particular trouble they would be well... These patients do not see that these various complaints are the only conscious form in which our culture permits them to express something which lies much deeper and is common to the various people who believe they suffer from this or that particular symptom. The common suffering is the alienation from oneself, from one's fellow men and women, and from nature; the awareness that life runs out like sand, and that one will die without having lived.

Here we shall be concerned primarily with erotic relationships, whether of the transient "romantic" kind or committed as "partnerships" (married or not). However, a similar existential sense of lack or *dukkha* (somewhat misleadingly translated as "suffering") may be experienced in all close and potentially needy relationships, as between parents and children, or emotionally dependent friendships.

And a similar diagnosis and treatment through emotional awareness practice likewise applies.

In the second half of the twentieth century the traditional, institutionalised and relatively stable model of marriage was displaced by the needy, restless individualism of high modernity, peeling off another layer of the existential onion in its search for authenticity at the heart. It has been supplanted by "partnership" in a committed relationship. Modernity is marked by an urge for intimacy which has become intense and compulsive, focussing upon "relationships", a word which, (like "partnership") assumed its present meaning only in the last fifty years or so.

The relationship is a unique phenomenon in that, unlike traditional marriage, it is totally disembedded from any external social conditions and exists only for itself. It must therefore accommodate all the emotional, intellectual and existential baggage of both parties often with unreasonably high mutual expectations. And it must do so in the midst of a speedy, agitated consumer society, (under the pressure, in the UK, of the longest working hours in Europe), and often with the demands of child-rearing, (which may well push parents apart rather than pulling them together).

We may note, in parenthesis, that if there is not too great a mutual neediness then this emotional exposure may be mitigated by practical arrangements which ensure that each partner is able to lead a separate and autonomous life *consistent with a loving relationship*. That is to say, the distance should be appropriate for sustaining the relationship and not for evading its challenges. Thus the Sufi poet Kahil Gibran wrote in *The Prophet*:

> Love one another, but make not a bond of love...
>
> Fill each other's cup, but drink not from the one cup...
>
> Stand together yet not too near together;

For the pillars of the temple stand apart.

And the oak tree and the cypress grow not in each other's shadow.

Nonetheless, whatever such practical adjustments may be made to reduce its pressures, to sustain an intimate relationship remains an emotionally demanding undertaking. Such demands are not obstacles or distractions in our Buddhist practice, just as our practice is more than a means of managing these demands. They are themselves our practice. In the following observation, Charlotte Joko Beck, that pioneer of contemporary "Ordinary Mind Zen", echoes a great many present-day Dharma teachers in all traditions:

> Relationships with people, especially close and trusting ones, are our best way to grow. In them we can see what our mind, our body, our senses and our thoughts really are. There is no way that is superior to relationships in helping us to see where we are stuck and what we're holding onto. As long as our buttons are being pushed we have a great chance to learn and grow. So a relationship is a great gift not because it makes us happy — it often doesn't — but because any intimate relationship, if we view it as practice, is the clearest mirror we can find.

However, we can only truly know a relationship to the extent that we deeply know ourselves, and this can be a long and arduous journey. The good news is that love motivates and inspires us to develop that deeper self-knowledge, without which love may perish.

No matter in what part of our life we are practicing in order to mature wisdom and compassion, the Dharmic diagnosis and treatment are essentially the same. So at this point essential re-reading will be found in the earlier "Talk Three" on the practice of Emotional Awareness, and also "Talk One" on the Lifelong Lawsuit with Reality. In the latter, at the end of the section entitled "The Lawsuit", I have touched upon the distinction between two opposing impulsions both of which, confusingly may be termed "desire". On the one hand there is the delusive, egocentric clinging and grasping whereby the self struggles to defend and enlarge its identity and sphere of control — and nowhere, on the personal level, more strongly than in close relationship. By contrast, there is the compassionate desire, moved by a sense of at-one-ness with the other, which selflessly seeks the other's well-being, and which manifests naturally from our True (or Buddha) Nature. In the more subtle instances great clarity of mind, cultivated by a sustained meditation practice, is needed to discern the difference. We can easily deceive ourselves as to our true motives, and nowhere is the warning in the *XinXinMing* more relevant than here: "Make a hair's breadth difference and Heaven and Earth are set apart." It is here that the shifting boundary runs between true love and *egoisme à deux*. This confusion surrounding the word "desire" in Buddhist teaching has been helpfully addressed in Mark Epstein's book *Open to Desire*.

The *Dukkha* of Relationships

In the blaze of erotic passion and romantic neediness we are customarily unaware how love thrives on *lack*. Or, as David Loy questions, "is it the reverse: does our *lack* thrive on love? We are not unaware that passion means suffering, but we imagine that such passion is nonetheless exciting and vital in a way ordinary life is not. Therefore we revel in pain, for all pain is endurable if we can see a reason for it and an end to it." In our heightened state of delusion we believe that the anxious self will at last find the ultimate in security and gratification — in terms of affection, recognition, appreciation, care and limitless sexual gratification — in brief, the end of existential fear.

Subsequently we begin to see that the other is not quite what we had imagined him or her to be — that is, someone ideally suited to gratify a whole range of our needs. We may feel angry, resentful and let down. We may even begin to realise that we committed to them for what we felt they could give us, instead of who they now appear to be, with all their "inadequacies". We want them to be different from what we now see they are. These dissonances commonly make themselves felt in annoying disagreements over money, ways of spending the time, the other's friends and family, and so on. There may be interminable discussion, reasoning and argument to persuade the other to change their inconvenient ways. As always the mentality is about "How can I fix that problem out there?"

Furthermore, this whole reaction will doubtless be going on in the other person. He or she becomes aware of their own needs not being adequately addressed by the other, who is at the same time making demands that threaten his or her own precariously fortified identity. Instead of being able to help in the vain attempt to win one's lifelong lawsuit with reality he or she appears, on the contrary, to be destabilising the project.

For example, she may want love, romance and tenderness before she can feel the confidence and self-assurance to let herself go. He, however, may be hell-bent on his own erotic passion, and unable to understand what he may see as her frigidity and romantic foibles.

If the couple do not split up, they may settle down to some unhappy mix of attempted control and autonomy. For example, one may attempt to maintain some control over the other so that his or her own needs are at least minimally satisfied. The other may, short of leaving, act as if they don't really need the other, emotionally or sexually. They may withdraw into a virtuous, cool, self-control — perhaps dedicating themselves to some "spiritual practice". In fact, they have deadened and repressed a vital part of themselves, (and maybe also have fallen into the trap of "spiritual by-passing").

There is a very different, possible accommodation between the couple, termed co-dependence. This indeed may have brought them together in the first place, and, far from being a cause of suffering, may make for a comfortable and agreeable lifelong relationship. There is here a more or less unconscious collusion; "I'll compensate you for ways in which you are emotionally intellectually and erotically incomplete, and you do the same for me." Traditionally this was socially built in, in the form of separate male and female roles, most notably that of the male breadwinner and the female homemaker. Social changes have now diminished the importance of such roles, but not the co-dependence arising from the male and female aspects of personality. The male has no need to develop the female side of his personality because his partner, playing the opposite hand, provides for him the entire female side of their marriage. Typically she may take care of the social side of their lifestyle, and provide the nurturing and emotional backup and lubrication in family and marriage. She may apparently play no more than a supportive role to the hard-edged structural functionalism of the male, though in fact holding the real power in the family.

Many life-long marriages are founded on co-dependence, and reckoned to be "successful". But, as with other kinds of "accommodations" which enable some people to "get through" life without too much suffering, the price of co-dependence is that it blocks either party from developing their full potential, that is, the masculine or feminine side of their personalities. Arguably, this can affect their potential for full spiritual maturity. I do recall a particularly interesting talk by Roshi Reb Anderson in this connexion. And another experienced Zen teacher once remarked to me that, as his male and female students ripened in their practice over the years, each tended gradually to become more rounded and complete in their manifestation of masculine and feminine characteristics. I shall return later to the *interdependence* of what has been called "the inner marriage".

Relationship as Spiritual Practice

Often, when in love, we may feel ourselves being pulled in opposing directions. On the one hand, we truly desire to connect with the other in an unconditional love arising from our Buddha Nature. On the other hand we may still cling to promoting and defending our self-image. It is at this crossing point that significant transformation of the self and of the relationship becomes possible.

Indeed, we may instinctively be drawn to a partner who is a worthy challenger, strong enough to ensure that we don't get away with what we want, and obliging us to confront the behaviours by which we seek to evade our underlying fear. At the same time to provide loving support whilst stimulating, provoking and nurturing in this way requires skill, honesty, and courage. A bit of playfulness and black comedy also goes a long way…

A valuable orientation in this maturation process is the so-called "inner marriage", whereby the man is enabled to develop his feminine side (*anima, yin*) and the women her masculine side (*animus, yang*). The *anima* (or Wisdom principle) has an inner, receptive quality, open to insight, creativity and oblique thinking, opening to life and accepting ourselves as we are, with a grounded physicality. The *animus* (or Compassion principle) has the opposite qualities — action-orientated, intellectual, visionary, structural, functionalist and so on.

In our still substantially patriarchal culture, the precarious self in each gender may feel threatened by the other. He may feel threatened by her "emotionality" and "irrationality" and respond with an aggressive, corrupted animus. She may feel devalued and mistreated by his macho culture and, in hardening herself against it, may cut herself off from her feminine (*yin*) power. Thus there may be obstacles on both sides to opening up and letting in the *anima* or *animus* of the other.

In the Tantric tradition of Tibetan Buddhism this inner marriage has an important place in spiritual maturation. The story is told of the great yogi Naropa, who believed that he understood not only the words but the inner meaning of the Dharma until he was confounded by a playful (and wrathful) dakini hag who taught him he was not yet as spiritually advanced as he had supposed. In Zen a similar role is played by the obscure old woman running the tea stall outside the monastery, lying in wait to trounce the supposedly omniscient Master.

From the practical point of view, returning to the pair of "worthy challengers" introduced above, the first step (as always in Dharma practice) is to look within — preferably in the most contemplative state that can be mustered. One can consider this looking within in three stages: Analysis, Contemplation, and Positive Dialogue.

Analysis

First, identify something which bothers you about your partner — some way he or she treats you and for which you blame them. Secondly, how do you experience this, feel it, interpret it? Thirdly, why does it bother you so much? (an affront, perhaps, to your dignity and autonomy?). Fourthly, what is there about you which causes this to get to you? (like, lack of confidence, feeling slighted by others). Here your emotional awareness practice will have made you familiar with your inner furniture and baggage; becoming intimate with this is surely one of the first undertakings in a Dharma practice, uncomfortable and disconcerting though it may be.

Working through the above steps we begin to see how anger and resentment is commonly born out of fear. And that fear is a key issue underlying most relationship difficulties. There is fear of being left alone, of being rejected, of being overwhelmed, of having our weaknesses exposed, of too much intimacy, of not getting what we want or losing what we have, and so on.

Contemplation

After this stage of analysis (which can, of course, be repeated as needs be) we come to the emotional awareness practice of becoming intimate with a workable feeling which has been identified in the previous paragraph, such as fear of being left alone (see "Talk Three — The Practice of Emotional Awareness"). This second, contemplative stage is perhaps the most important in securing a successful outcome for the process as a whole.

Positive Dialogue

The third stage (though there will probably, of course, be several such episodes) has been called "The No-Fault Listening Zone". Even if your partner is not following the kind of practice set out here, providing you are undertaking the necessary work on yourself you can still initiate work with them in a positive and unthreatening way. This encourages them to reciprocate, and some kind of positive dialogue becomes possible. What were once implacably defended desires can become negotiable preferences. I am reminded of the following parable by the Taoist sage Chuang-Tzu:

If a man is crossing a river

And an empty boat collides with his own skiff,

Even though he be a bad tempered man

He will not become very angry.

But if he sees a man in the boat,

He will shout at him to steer clear.

And if his shout is not heard, he will shout again.

And yet again, and begin cursing,

If you can empty your own boat

Crossing the river of the world,

No one will oppose you,

No one will seek to harm you.

The No Fault Listening Zone may be set up when both parties are feeling well disposed — or, more audaciously, after some all-too-familiar row (in which case the process can reveal what lies beneath). Each takes it in turn to tell the truth about their experience and the hard time they are having with the relationship. They both agree not to assign blame. The one who is speaking is not to be interrupted. The other remains silent and tries hard to understand, and he or she may repeat back in their own words what they believe they have heard.

With this work it is possible that with a more realistic picture of their relationship one or both parties may decide that they are no longer sufficiently in love to sustain a partnership with any mutually acceptable degree of commitment, and they should part. Such a decision, of course, is not to be taken hastily, and much depends on the maturity and extent of self-knowledge of the couple. We live in a fast food culture in which patience and forgiveness are not prominent virtues. Some sense of commitment, of being in it for the long haul, can provide a helpful supportive framework, like sharing a home, marrying, and having children. The ultimate commitment is that of undertaking an intimate lifelong journey together, each maturing in the light of the other... as well as maturing in their own light. Here there is no sacramental guarantee — only the playfulness of those who have learnt to live lightly in an impermanent and insubstantial world. And people may, of course, change and evolve away from one another in this world of arrivals and departures.

A committed, long-term relationship of the kind I have outlined, ripening in unconditional love, can be a spiritual journey in a profound and yet non-explicit sense. It will draw upon what each partner has made of the maturing potential of other areas of their lives, including contemplative alone-ness. It will especially draw on how far they have learnt to accept — and even to love — themselves, and are thus freed to love others. One's partner may have traits which we might prefer were otherwise, but we learn not to view these personally; it is the whole person whom we love, beyond our likes and dislikes. This is an unconditional love which has been cleansed of our need to perceive the other in any self-serving way. This is the *suchness* of Zen, beyond wanting this and rejecting that. We relate to the other in the spirit of Dogen's quotation that "every creature covers the ground it stands on — no more nor no less. It never falls short of its completeness". Such a relationship embodies the Two Truths, as they are sometimes called in Buddhism, reflecting the oneness of form and emptiness. As Shunryu Suzuki playfully put it: "You're perfect as you are; but there's still room for improvement...."

Sexuality as Spiritual Practice

The more profane may well chortle at the above heading. "No sex, please, we're Buddhists!" The fact that sex so rarely appears, except in passing, in Western Buddhist teaching and practice is evidence of the enduring, taken-for-granted grip of the Asian monastic tradition. And yet we live in a culture saturated with sexuality. Sex is commodified both in itself (e.g. as pornography) and as an advertising lure. Moreover the preoccupation with sexual gratification helps to fill the void left in a highly individualistic culture in which traditional mores are in decline. "Good sex" has become a human right, essential for self-esteem.

The sexual drive undoubtedly differs between individuals — those who have weak "engines" and strong "brakes" may even wonder what all the fuss is about. At its most powerful — and especially when embellished with romantic love — it sweeps all before it, amounting to a veritable possession, a force of nature so overwhelming as to appear irresistible, so that it feels that sex is exploiting the helpless self rather than vice versa. Unsurprisingly it has aroused much fear, individually and socially, and been subject to all manner of controls, ranging from personal repression and guilt, through punitive moral judgement, to a fearsome range of religious and patriarchal taboos and prohibitions (particularly directed at the sinful daughters of Eve).

Sex is, of course, simply a strong biological drive, neither "good" nor "bad" in itself.

On the one hand, it can powerfully (if temporarily) fill our sense of *lack*, incorporated as a major addictive resource in our lifelong lawsuit with life. This is what Ven. Sangharakshita termed *neurotic* sex. Sexual passion can impart a seemingly omnipotent self-identity. This is particularly so where it is exploited to dominate and control another — or to be dominated by another. In a relationship it commonly supercharges some of the dissonances already referred to in this talk. "I have my own life to live — not to be exploited as some sexual chattel. And I'll let him /her know this by not letting them have their way just when they feel like it. And, who knows? – I might get around to enjoying *my* sexuality somewhere else..."

On the other hand, providing that sexual chemistry is not predominant in bringing a couple together, passionate love-making can wipe clear the clogged, self-protecting windows of perception, softening and opening deep, selfless feeling for the beloved. For in Buddhism the *physicality* of the emotions receives full acknowledgement. And, in a different context, the Tantrayana surely bears witness to the spiritual potential of the erotic. Nonetheless, "a healthy sex life" is by no means essential for a committed relationship, as becomes clear in later years when the sexual urge diminishes and the love which sustains and delights the couple stands free of its earlier erotic highlighting.

It is noteworthy that the contrasting emotions in the above two paragraphs further exemplify the distinction I made earlier between the two radically different meanings of "desire".

In Zen Buddhism we find a general absence of concern for relationships and sexuality which presumably reflects its cultural and monastic origins, whereas in some of the Tibetan traditions sexuality receives a richer and more complex treatment. The asceticism of the Theravada is typically reflected in the aversion therapy of the well-known meditation on the underlying loathsomeness of the body of one's would-be lover. For further reading in Asian Buddhist sexuality see *Lust for Enlightenment: Buddhism and Sex*, by John Stevens (1990) and *Red Thread: Buddhist Approaches to Sexuality* by Bernard Faure (1998).

For most Western lay practitioners the most significant teaching on sexuality is the Third Precept. This has been expressed as not doing harm to others by liaising with someone who is already in a committed relationship, or, more comprehensively (and usefully), not allowing oneself to be invaded by sexual greed. Fucking a body without significantly and fully relating to the person embodied is a denial of their humanity. This may of course, be mutual (and mutually debasing) in an *égoïsme à deux*, but most reprehensible of all in the seduction of a weaker by a stronger personality (as may be the case in the teacher- student role).

The relationship between love and sexuality is, of course, tangled and complex, and there is no necessary connexion between them. Love and mutual respect need time and opportunity to ripen, letting sex take its natural course within that context. Allowing erotic chemistry alone to become the basis, for a relationship is very likely to end in tears, with the waning of the original intensity of the *affaire*.

A situational rather than a literal ethic — see my "Talk Four" — is particularly important in respect of the Third Precept. In all intimate relationship (and especially when purple with passion), the self is especially fearful, needy, protective and aggressive when faced with transgression and betrayal. There is ready resort to a punitive righteousness in place of the wise and reflective compassion required in what are usually more complex situations than may first appear. And even when the ethical course of action is clear, as in the need to end an affair, patience will be necessary. An act of will, with the accompanying emotional suppression and anguished guilt, may provide an instant solution but only at the cost of storing up trouble for the future, since the underlying problems remain unresolved. Contemplative practices like emotional awareness are needed to "work through" feelings of bitterness, loss and resentment, and this takes patience and support. When the fruit has had time to ripen on the tree, it can be plucked without bringing down the whole tree.

There is a prevailing obsession with sexual intercourse as some kind of absolute in an intimate relationship — "Yes, but did they ever *really* become lovers, and, if so, when?" Nonetheless, a strong relationship can survive and even mature in the face of sexual betrayal and failure. In this connection the three steps of a forgiveness practice may be helpful.

First, this is not about forgiving what the other has *done*, but forgiveness of the *person*. Rather than just telling oneself to "Drop it! Let it go!" it may be more helpful to acknowledge an unwillingness to forgive and a strong, gutsy preference to go on nursing resentment, bitterness and rage. Secondly, actually open up to those feelings ("No one should have to put up with this..." etc.) and become intimate with them without letting them carry you away. For the present, own, as your own responsibility, those feelings which are causing you so much grief and acknowledge their resolution *as your own task*. Attend to the tenseness and the other distresses of the body. Finally, sooner or later it will become possible to perceive more clearly what might be driving the other, and understanding and forgiveness — even voiced in words — may become possible.

Whether or not caught up in an impassioned (or threatening) situation, it is important for all followers of the Way to become fully aware of their sexuality, however manifested, to ensure that it is not by-passed in their practice, and, on the contrary, is treated as a spiritual resource. This applies no less to the chastity option, pursued with clarity and honesty in the face of an uncomprehending present-day culture.

Roshi Reb Anderson offers the following endorsement of the above contention, as welcoming as it is rare from a Zen teacher:

> Intimacy with your sexuality is the ultimate fulfilment of the bodhisattva precept of no sexual greed. Intimacy with sexuality means that there is a deep understanding of no separation between self and other. This is using sexuality to purify sexuality. Realizing this intimacy is like putting the last piece into place in a jigsaw puzzle; it is like the moment when you finally learn a great poem by heart.

Erich Fromm is quoted from his essay in *Zen Buddhism and Psycho-analysis*, edited by T.D.Suzuki (Souvenir Press, 1974). Charlotte Joko Beck has a substantial treatment of relationships in her book *Everyday Zen: Love and Work* (Harper Collins/Thorsons, 1997). The David Loy quotation is from "Trying to become real: a Buddhist critique of some social heresies", *International Philosophical Quarterly*, 32(4) Dec.1992. That by Reb Anderson is from *Being Upright: Zen Meditation and the Bodhisattva Precepts* (Rodmell Press, Berkeley, USA, 2001, p118).

In preparing this talk I have found John Welwood's *Love and Awakening: Discovering the Sacred Path of Intimate Relationship* (Harper Perennial, 1997) particularly valuable.

Talk Six — Using the Self to Transcend the Self

This paper summarises the ideas and practices introduced in Papers One and Three (above), and extends them to enquiry and contemplative practice to do with the phenomenon of the self. Enlarged and supported by the other "Talks" these three offer a comprehensive guide to the practice of an "Everyday Buddhism" in the Zen tradition, as exemplified in the reading list which is also available.

Here are the main points covered in Talks One and Three, to which the reader should refer for more details. They are offered here rather as an aide-memoire.

The impermanence and insubstantiality of phenomena create existential insecurity, angst and a sense of *lack* in the individual. The response is typically to kindle the "Three Fires" of anger, greed and ignorance. The fearful self seeks to evade everything which threatens its precarious security and to desire everything which can fortify it — ingrained emotional patterns, root beliefs, behaviours and lifestyles. This process takes place in a social milieu. Some find a stronger identity through a sense of belongingness to a larger entity — family, community, race, nation and so on. Others may be more concerned to stand out, to make their mark, and to be fortified by the esteem in which they are held. Beyond genetic inheritance (plus karmic rebirth?) and the powerful conditioning of childhood upbringing, we each build up our own distinctive personality — some more fearful and heavily defended than others. To become fully aware of the shaping and character of one's personality, and particularly of one's "emotional furniture", is a major requirement of Buddhist practice.

In his parable of the *Two Arrows* the Buddha distinguished between the pain experienced by the self when its integrity and identity is somehow threatened (e.g. a bereavement, or a cancer diagnosis), and, on the other hand, the particular response, which can differ widely between individuals when struck by much the same affliction. In a sense these are all evasions, although in our "fix it" culture the affliction may be more or less resolved by some objective instrumentality (anti-depressants and psychotherapy, chemotherapy and surgery, in the two examples). Typical "evasions" include denial, anger, blame, busyness, rationality, projection, and exclusive dependence on an objective fix. However, none of these evasions can, in the long run, fortify the threatened self sufficiently or for long enough. The helpless frustration, fear and anger which then arises is what the Buddha termed *dukkha* (rather misleadingly translated as "suffering"). Hubert Benoit graphically characterized this process as a lifelong and ultimately unwinnable lawsuit against reality.

However, the above Dharmic process of the shaping of a self would be no more than a caricature without clarification of the nature of desire, about which there appears to be some confusion. It is necessary to distinguish between attachment (that is, the need of the small self to attach itself to something which will confirm and strengthen it) and the "authentic" desire which arises from our undeluded Buddha Nature (or True Self, or Authentic Self). Thus, we may experience a desire to help others. On the one hand, such a desire may serve to inflate the self (e.g. a sense of superiority over the one who is helped, and giving self-prestige and a meaning to life). On the other hand, it may be a compassionate and selfless response to another's misfortune and need. Awareness of these very different and often mixed emotions requires the clarity engendered by meditation. For an extended discussion see Mark Epstein's *Open to Desire: The Truth About What the Buddha Taught* (New York: Gotham Books, 2006).

"Everyday Buddhism" uses the above experiences of the self as a means to transform our experience of the self, effecting a radical shift in consciousness. The practice of a physically rooted emotional awareness works to this end. "Emotional" here is used to include thinking as well as feeling, as with "mind" (or "heart-mind") as commonly translated from the Chinese. Awareness of the pains, griefs and discomfitures of the self is particularly valuable — "where the shoe pinches". Thus it is common in inner-path spiritualities for the practitioner to be exhorted to greet misfortunes as guests, as potentially transformative experiences, whereby straw may be spun into gold. To respond to a misfortune as a positive challenge does of course involve a reversal of our ingrained reaction.

In emotional awareness practice there are various ways in which we can become intimate with the pain of a misfortune. We may, for example, use our imaginations where necessary to conjure up some particularly acute experience of the discomfiture. Meditatively we may ask ourselves repeatedly "How does it *feel?*" Most important of all is profoundly to sense emotional pain in the body.

Through emotional awareness, on and off the cushion and in retreat situations, the clinging to this and the rejection of that begins to slacken, and increasingly we settle instead into the experience of *suchness*, of the just-how-it-isness of time, place and persons. As its says in the *XinXinMing* "When the mind makes no distinctions, all things are as they are." The major turn about is when it dawns upon us that both we and the world are basically okay just as they are; we awaken to our authentic or Buddha nature, and it is said that "the real practice" begins there, when we leave the realm of "belief" and enter that of "faith". We become more at ease with our selves and hence with others. No longer self-absorbed, we are freed into compassionate service.

And yet at the same time we are more deeply aware of the suffering in the world and of the world. Everything is okay, and yet grievously not so. These two contradictory truths, this paradox, can only be lived, and cannot be encompassed by logic chopping perturbations. Thus, as Shunryu Suzuki remarked to one of his students: "You're fine just as you are, but there's plenty of room for improvement". More pithily: nothing matters, everything matters.

The Self as a Process

The above prepares us for a further enquiry into the self. Ajahn Chah, the great Thai Forest meditation teacher, said that "To say there is a self is untrue. To say there is no self is untrue. What, then, is true?" The existence (or otherwise) of the self thus appears as an enigma, a paradox, for the logical mind. To claim that it does not exist has created problems which have long preoccupied philosophers. And yet no one, from the ancient sages to contemporary neuro-scientists, has in fact been able to establish its existence in any meaningful way. Wittgenstein classified it with such other mysterious substantive nouns such as "time", which are necessary to our discourse but which can never be specifically identified.

The Buddha was once asked by the wanderer Vacchagotta whether the self existed. But he remained silent. So Vacchagotta asked him whether the self did not exist. And again the Buddha remained silent. Subsequently he explained to Ananda that had he replied to either question with a simple negative or affirmative he would have misrepresented his position. (Note that his silence is not intended to point to some mysterious and incomprehensible absolute self.)

It is rather that the Buddha saw the self as a *process,* and not as a constant entity subjected to a succession of experiences which might change only its secondary qualities. He saw the "problem" of the self as being our very preoccupation with whether the self does or does not exist as missing the point. Buddhist thought spells out the above process in various possible ways. Most notable is the causal connectedness expressed in the Five Aggregates:- sensation, feeling,

126

perception/ volition, conception, and consciousness. Another such formula sets out the principle of causality in twelve links — the *nidana* chain of "dependent arising". The Buddha maintained that there is no constant and unchanging self having these experiences; there is only the experiencing, constantly changing from one moment to the next. It is the continuity of experience which gives rise to the illusion of a self. Moreover, this *process* is essentially a bodily experience. The more deeply the body is explored, the more it dissolves into energy, losing the reassuring idea of solidity which the fearful self has imposed on it.

This is our perception when we are freed of existential fear and feel more at one with the universe, becoming then a truly self-less person — our authentic or Buddha nature. Our sense of self then becomes no more than a convenient label, a pragmatic convenience. In contrast to this "Big Self" is the "Small Self", conceived as a solid, if precarious, entity. This is the self that conducts the lifelong and unwinnable lawsuit with the reality of insubstantiality and impermanence.

Exploring the Self

With the clarity engendered by meditation, each of us can dispassionately observe the phenomenon of our self, and we may even distinguish several such selves, such as a top dog self which endeavours to control a self-indulgent bottom dog self. This observer (sometimes archly called The One Who Knows) enables us to *observe* the driven "small self" without being *owned* by it. It has been variously called Big Mind, the Big Self, or No-Self. We can explore the self with a two pronged kind of awareness. sensing when identification with self is strong (i.e. delusion) and when it is weak (i.e. Big Mind), and what each feels like. In Jack Kornfield's words: "The creation of self is a process that can be observed moment to moment. It arises when we identify with some part of our experience and call it "me" or "mine". We can see what it feels like when the identification with self is strong, when it is weak, and even when it is absent". A Self remains, but it is a No Self (Big Mind) in that in that it is no longer significantly driven by the Three Fires.

It is a valuable exercise to recall typical situations when you have a strong sense of your delusive, assertive (and vulnerable) self. How does it feel in the body? How do others respond? What would it feel like in that situation without that strong self-identification? For example, when you are criticised, or disparaged. How do you feel — anxious, angry, upset — and how would it feel if you didn't identify? Contrariwise, recall other situations when clinging to your selfhood is mild or even absent. How does it feel? How is it when your response is relaxed, easy, and even playful?

But resist any temptation to try to define No-self, to solidify it or attach to it. This is the customary threat of spiritual materialism ("Talk Four").

On a highly disciplined and silent retreat the delusive self is restricted in its self-affirming freedoms: the schedule supplants choice of this or that; mindfulness supplants day dreaming, and so on. In place of the customary agitated this-versus-that state of mind, there is, much more than usual, simply the mind of bare awareness. Such a retreat therefore offers a unique opportunity. Awareness of the self can substantially take the place of our usual identification with it. Other potentially fruitful situations are when the self's laboriously created fortifications are seriously breached, so that it is unable to manifest itself as previously, as with physical disablement, or loss of prestige when unemployed, or the formidable combination of these disablements associated with old age.

The foregoing kind of shift in awareness may be intensively experienced as Unity Consciousness — self-world unity, or

"One Mind" experiences. This represents a radical reversal of small self's self-absorbed, acute-angled view of the world (and of itself), analogous to being turned right side up. As Dogen observed in his metaphor of the boat and the shore, we wake up to the realisation that it is the boat that is moving and not, as we had supposed, the shore.

This is a step in the direction of *kensho*, when "body and mind drop off". Here there is a unique sense of the absence of self — only experience remains. Examples from Chan Master John Crook: finding no-one looking at the face in the mirror; walking down a street and suddenly finding oneself (necessarily) "returning" when trying to cross in traffic; seeing a rare bird and discovering no one doing the seeing. (For more on "enlightenment" see my "Talk Two".)

Together with opening to suchness, a well practiced habit of observing (small) self without identifying with it can, in the context of emotional awareness and a meditation discipline, make for a life more easeful, less self-absorbed, more actively compassionate, and free of the underlying fear and anxiety which commonly haunts the human condition.

Talk Seven — Don't Know Mind and Storehouse Consciousness

"Don't Know Mind" is our open, curious, playful and exploring mind, coming forth from the suchness of experience and no longer attached to *this* or rejecting *that* and clinging to self-need. The sequence of previous "talks" in this series offer some cognitive exploration of the Dharma, pointing to "Don't Know Mind". We now more fully enter the realm of insight, which strikes us as matter of *fact* (in contrast to some self-conceived *idea*). However, it would be wrong to make any sharp distinction between thought, feeling and insight. Insightful wisdom slowly ripens the personality over a lifetime, in which the shift from belief to faith is particularly significant (see "Talk Two"). And many different experiences of an awakening awareness can contribute to that ripening process. For example, on reading Susan Murphy's *Upside Down Zen*, can we not but feel a sense of wonder, spaciousness and awe when we come across sentences like "Time is the narrow footpath in eternity which we walk in our magical, momentary bodies"?

"Upside Down Zen" is one of the many metaphors designed to point out that our habitual ways of experiencing life are the opposite of how it would be if we were freed of what Blake called our "mind forged manacles". Likewise Darlene Cohen calls her book *Turning Suffering Inside Out*. And Dogen draws our attention to the fact that it is not the shore moving in relation to the boat (as we commonly experience phenomena), but the contrary. And, again, Shunryu Suzuki refers to the acute angled view of the deluded self, surveying the world as if from its centre. In the Pali Canon this phenomenon of cognitive illusions is called *vipalasas* (inversions). Bhikkhu Bodhi explains:

These inversions infest the entire process of cognition, so that instead of seeing things as they really are, we see them in ways that are quite the opposite. In the impermanent we see permanence; in what is bound up with pain and suffering we see glimmers of pleasure ... The *vipallasas* twist our cognition and thereby send us on an inherently insatiable quest for gratification.

The paradoxes which lie at the heart of spiritual experience confound the neat logic to which the insecure self holds fast. In the words of the Chan poem *XinXinMing*, "What is the same as what is not; what is not is the same as what is. Until you have grasped this you will have no peace of mind. One thing is all things; all things are one thing. If this is so for you there is no need to worry about enlightenment." Likewise, koans present paradoxical problems that cannot be solved rationally. For example, how, without getting wet, would you retrieve a stone which lies on the ocean floor? The method is to immerse yourself in the saying and see how it changes you.

In his book B*ring me the Rhinoceros and other Zen Koans which will Change your Life*, John Tarrant includes a koan about "The Red Thread": "Songyuan asked: 'Why can't clear-eyed Bodhisattvas sever the red thread?'" The red thread signifies desire and passion, and especially, it appears, erotic passion ("It's the red thread between your legs" said Songyuan). Typically the self makes one or other of two kinds of response. On the one hand it may seek gratification by a mindless immersion in desire. On the other hand (and a common spiritual response) it may seek to repress desire, virtuously and righteously controlling it by means of ethical commandments and precepts enforced literally and absolutely. Tarrant observes that "the red thread is always tangled and resists the simplification of life into formulae ... Erotic connections turn life upside down, and when life is too right, turning things upside down can be a good thing. This koan resists the totalitarian impulse in spiritual paths ...

Everyone has some sainthood possible, and the unfolding of their goodness might sometimes be through transgressions, through what is wild and imperfect in them ... The point of this koan might be found in truly living your life rather than living it perfectly or even respectably."

As Philip Epstein has pointed out in his book *Open to Desire*, there appears to be some confusion among Buddhists who commonly condemn desire as if it invariably referred to delusive attachment and acquisitiveness. But what of the desire springing from our authentic (Buddha) nature? Is our desire to help another moved by a righteous and patronising self-importance or by spontaneous feelings of compassion? How much self-gratifying lust may there be in a relationship and how much selfless love? Surely a problematic bit of both in all these and similar instances? The passions are indeed our Buddha nature. This does not make for a secure and orderly world of certainties and predictabilities. Nor a self-indulgent world of personal and institutional greed and aggressiveness.

When the self has quietened down a little, and the "ten thousand things" are strongly manifesting themselves then the Don't Know Buddha Mind can come forth — perhaps as a dream, or a piece of music, or maybe in the words of a poem which creatively frustrate our attempt to make sense of things. Like Nagata Koi's haiku:

> How lonely it is
>
> cultivating the stone leeks
>
> in this world of dreams

Or it may be just the luminous intensity of the supermarket checkout queue being the supermarket checkout queue. Whatever it may be, the injunction translated by Alan Watts from the Chan poem "Trust in the Heart" is worth attention:

> Follow your nature and accord with the Way

Saunter along and stop worrying.

When your thoughts are tied you spoil what is genuine.

Do not be antagonistic to the senses;

When you are not, it turns out to be the same as complete awakening.

The wise person does not strive;

The ignorant tie themselves up.

If you work on your mind with your mind

How can you avoid complete confusion?

What we experience as the solidity of phenomena (including the self) turns out to be no more than particular mental constructions ("form"), like the meaning of the little black shapes on this page. The artist, the physicist, or a blind person may each have a different "picture" of a piece of rock, ranging from its molecular structure to its tactile texture or its play of light. Always there is "form", but never any immutable and solid reality. "Form is only emptiness, emptiness only form", as the Heart Sutra reminds us, and Thomas Cleary has likened the paradoxical relationship between the two to that of matter and energy — you can't have one without the other. Investigation leads us finally to nothing other than "experience" — consciousness. But consciousness is always conscious of some specific experience. So can you find mind — consciousness — that is not connected thus? Is this the "Mind" conceived by the Mahayana philosophers — the "Big Mind"? As the XinXinMing reminds us, "the more you talk about it, the more you think about it, the further from it you go." Surely "uncertainty" and the "unknown"(as we first experience them) are the only things we can, ultimately, rely upon, and in our wholehearted acceptance of them we are freed of fear.

Storehouse Consciousness (*Alayavijnana*)

Many years ago I accepted the view taught to me of the self "guarding the senses" and "taking refuge" in the precepts, lest existential insecurity and a sense of "lack" impels the self to burn with the Three Fires of hatred, grasping and ignorance. This is the view of the delusive self ignorant and cutting itself off from a universal consciousness. This is how it may feel when the sense of a separate self is quite strong, and the energies are not overwhelming.

But later, with a wider experience if life, I realised, however, that there are times when the self feels itself out of control and "invaded", "overwhelmed" and "carried away" by emotional energies — "forgetting itself" in aggressive rage, irresistible greed, or helpless lust. Or, on the contrary, it may be a powerful impulse to self-sacrifice for others or some other numinous insight arising from unity consciousness. For better or worse, small self has done something (like a meditative retreat, or falling in love), or had something done to it, which triggers an invasion of karmic proclivities beyond its customary consciousness. "I really don't know what made me do it" may be said out of a selfless courage as out of a self-consuming rage.

Thus the demon lover, the mass murderer and the saint all may open to a collective consciousness, whether tainted or uncorrupted, and the power and charisma of all of them is the wonder of the many folk, who keep things decently under control. As to the saint, a profound "opening" to the untainted collective unconsciousness may still leave intact karmically uncleansed aspects of that consciousness. This may amount to the "spiritual inflation" of ego, as Jung called it.

The above reflections point experientially to the existence of a truly universal consciousness which embraces delusion as well as enlightenment. To understand this consciousness, which is better described as "storehouse" or "base" consciousness (*alayavijana*) some introduction to the Yogacara school of Mahayana Buddhism is necessary (most readily available through the *Lankavatara Sutra* — a foundation text of Chan/Zen). The term "Yogacara" reminds us of its origins in meditative insight, rather than being the fanciful metaphysical edifice which some scholars like Edward Conze were inclined to regard it. For our purpose the alternative name of Vijnananavada — "Mind Only" is more helpful, however.

As a theory of knowledge the Yogacara occupies a middle way between the so-called Hinayana and the Madhyamika associated with Nagarjuna. Whereas the Hinayana postulates the existence of an objective reality, the Madhyamaka has been laid open to a charge of nihilism — "the dialectical dissolution of everything", as Conze nicely puts it. As noted earlier in this "talk", meditative enquiry leads us to an awareness of pure consciousness, of mind without a thinker. For the Yogacara everything perceptible is only mind (*cittamatra*); things *are* consciousness, *are* mind; that is the only safe assertion we can make of them. Perception is in fact no more than a process of imagination which creates in us the picture of the supposed objects. In the words of the *Lankavatara Sutra*:: "All is but mind. Mind makes its appearance in two ways: as the object to be grasped, and as the grasper (the subject.) There is no self, and nothing of the nature as a self."

At the heart of Buddhist psychology are the *skandhas*, a process whereby individual consciousness is created successively through sensation, feeling, perception (discrimination between good, bad and indifferent feelings) and volition, creating mental formations or concepts (*samskaras*), aggregating into consciousness.

The Yogacara set out to explain the origin of the *samskaras*, that is, the impulsive drives, cognitive patterns and karmic accumulations out of which a sense of self identity is constructed. The foundation is an oceanic Storehouse Consciousness. In this float the karmic impressions (*vasana*) or karmic seeds occasioned and left behind by past individuals. A function of the *alayavijnana* is that of thought*t* consciousness (*manovijnana*) which has a built-in urge to present itself in the ideated sense world in the form of karmic seeds which individuate into an entity (*manas*). This is the seat and motive power of a separate ego, the controlling centre which endeavours to maintain a strong sense of self using the karmic impulses provided by *manovijnana*. An analogy is a coiled piece of rope (provided by *manovijnana*) and its recognition as a snake by *manas*. Each individuated self again ideates its own private world which affirms its identity, but which also generates new karmic seeds which sink into the *alayavijnana*. A fanciful image suggests that the incoming impulses through the sense organs are like a perfume that scents the storehouse, creating seeds which grow into complex associative structures.

Meditation can lead to a turning around (*paravritti*) exposing the reality behind our hitherto dominant self-centredness, the "cleaning" of our karma, and our buried *individual* consciousness as a dimension of the universal unconsciousness. Such an enlightenment reveals the *amalvijnana* or untainted — "immaculate" — character of *alayavijnana* in contrast to the delusive appearance of *alayavijnana* described above. "All shall be well and all manner of thing shall be well", proclaims the mystic.

However, beyond that, we may also experience the more universal dimension itself, in terms of past lives and the many planes of existence. Practitioners may, for example, notice the spontaneous emergence of forgotten scenes from childhood and jumbled scenes of unknown people and strange places. They may be disconcerted by powerful feelings of rage or grief beyond anything previously experienced. As storehouse consciousness opens we may experience the many planes of existence, from the heavenly to the hellish. In his book *The Wise Heart* Jack Kornfield recounts his own experiences:

I have spent joyful hours listening to what seemed like celestial music sung by luminous beings, and seen a hundred forms of sacred groves and temples. At other times, when the realm of animals arose, I actually felt myself as a salmon, a crow, or an ant ... At other times I experienced the universal dimension of suffering, where the imagery is of loss and destruction. I sat for days on retreat as a hundred spontaneous images of death arose. I saw my body killed and stabbed and trampled in war, or lying helpless on a hundred sickbeds with diseases, or dying from an accident, a fall, a blow ... Sometimes these images were personal and individual, as if they were my own memories. Sometimes they felt more archetypal, as if the nature of life and death was displaying itself to me. At this point in my training I had developed a strong base of mindfulness and equanimity to meet these images wisely. My teacher encouraged me to steady my attention and rely on the space of awareness — he called this a training for equanimity at death" (p156).

Through meditation, and also through dreams and dream-like states, we may bring the delusive aspect of storehouse consciousness into full consciousness — where it can be transformed into the pure consciousness of our authentic (Buddha) nature. We can start with awareness into any area of suffering in our life and, if sufficiently penetrating, can follow it down into the previously hidden storehouse consciousness. Where is it felt most strongly in the body? What are the underlying feelings, images and beliefs that hold it in place? With profound intention we discover these instincts and drives to be the stuff of illusion, and we are released from them.

Even if we prove unable personally to open to profound meditative insights into storehouse consciousness, nonetheless, as Kornfield observes, "past lives teaching {in itself} serves two important psychological functions. When the suffering and pleasure in our life is attributed to our past lives

– and intentional behaviours – anxiety about a capricious, chaotic fate is eased. This perspective can bring acceptance, detachment and grace in facing life's difficulties. Secondly, rebirth teachings can bring greater care with our actions out of concern for the results they may produce in future rebirths" (p158).

Indeed, it has been suggested that, at least in part, the Yogacara may have arisen to provide an adequate explanation of the seeming contradiction between *anatta* and the doctrine of rebirth. For it is not a self that is reborn, but a constellation of karmic impulses, recallable under hypnosis or meditative trance, as in the above testimony (particularly recommended is Roger J Woolger's *Other Lives, Other Selves* (Crucible, 1990). Thus, the Dogen scholar, Hee-Jin Kim, maintains that "the store-consciousness is by far the most sophisticated concept innovated by the Buddhists in response to criticism of the idea of no-self; indeed, it almost envisions a self- surrogate, yet this differs, or allegedly differs, from any immutable, self-identical substratum of the self" (*Eihei Dogen: Mystical Realist*, p112).

Even though we may be unable personally to access it, knowing of storehouse consciousness, in both its individual and universal (collective) dimensions, presents us with an awesome reminder of how limited and self-absorbed is our customary experience – a reminder in confronting our death, as well as amplifying our faith.

It also enlarges our perception of the tragic drama of human history – the socio-historical charging of millions of individual wills, generation after generation. Storehouse consciousness is the source underlying and driving our conscious lives, as well as the hidden heart of our possibilities. It is this which supercharges history, driving peoples to commit atrocities against their neighbours which they would have found unimaginable in times of peace.

Finally, it is most important not to fall into a reification of store-consciousness. The Yogacara is careful not to affirm mind-only as itself some kind of ultimate reality. It is essential not to envision and cling to *Alayavijnana* as a receptacle of permanence and substance, instead of the transient experience which it is.

Talk Eight — How to be Kind

"Love" has so many different meanings; and "compassion" can feel lofty and remote. But "kindness" has a heartfelt warmth and spontaneity about it. "Kindness is my religion", proclaimed the Dalai Lama, so let us upgrade it from its modest and personal connotations. *Metta,* translated as "loving kindness", is after all one of the four *BrahmaViharas* or "blessed abodes", up there with compassion, equanimity and empathetic joy.

Who is it that wants to be Kind?

Before hastening to discover how we can acquire this precious quality of kindness it will be helpful to reflect a little on "Why do I want to be kind? "

Adrift on impermanence and insubstantiality, this fearful self struggles to establish an approved and affirming identity, above all in righteousness — the being good and right — and in being kind. As David Loy has observed of the stories we like to tell ourselves (1). "Our identities are constructed from what we detest as well as what we love... We prefer the orientation of a moral code, even if we don't follow it, to the disorientation of life without one." For example, helping others can make us feel good (and also superior to them), and win the social approval and self-esteem so much craved in maintaining a strong self-identity. In fact, such self-serving motivation tends to make us less serviceable to the helped who may, correspondingly, feel that they are being robbed of their self-esteem. To paraphrase Chekhov: "If you see someone coming towards you with the determination to be kind, make off in all haste in the opposite direction!"

This, however, is not the whole story. To stop there would be a misanthropic caricature of humanity. We commonly call the above sense of self a "small" self, a deluded expression of an authentic self. This latter is termed our "buddha nature" or, in Zen jargon, "Big Mind". (We can leave aside here the question of the nature of the self, which is treated in Talk Seven: "Using the Self to Transcend the Self"). Our authentic selfless self is moved by a natural and spontaneous kindness wholly responding to and at one with the needs of others.

Adequately to distinguish these two underlying kinds of motivation requires the cultivation of considerable insight, to see through the stories we tell ourselves about ourselves. Here, as elsewhere in these tricky realms, a logical, and earnest sensibility cannot take us far... It were better to accept our limitations, love ourselves and do our best.

Kindness, Intentionality and the Will

Traditionally Buddhism proceeds through three stages of training. Before clear seeing (*samadhi*) and insightful wisdom (*vipassana*) there is work to be done on *sila*, or moral observance. This involves restraint, aided by cognitive knowledge and personal reflection: "To study Buddhism is to study the self" is the first step (and an enduring practice) emphasised by the Buddha and all successive teachers. Thus we learn to recognise the existential pressures which move us to unkindness, reflect upon their consequences for ourselves and others, and endeavour to exercise the prudent and skilful restraint of which the moral precepts remind us. For example. where possible, we should avoid people and situations which arouse in us feelings of enmity so strong that we are not yet able to handle them positively. In other words, don't water the weeds. Some Westerners, hot in pursuit of insight and enlightenment, may be inclined to deny these so-called preliminaries the attention they deserve. Moreover cognitive understanding and conceptual reflection — the realm of belief — are not so sharply divided from insight as may be supposed, in the often slow but steady growth of the one into the other.

The other side of restraint is aspiration. What is sometimes termed "basic Buddhism", is replete with virtues like the five ethical precepts, the perfections — the *paramitas* — and the four great vows of Chan practice. The foregoing is the practice of intentionality, which is there to remind and inspire us as to what we are truly endeavouring to do. To frame some half dozen personal intentions, reflecting our knowledge of our self and its failings, is a useful reminder to have before us. However, although "May I be kind in all my dealings", for example, may provide a helpful reminder they do not specifically tell us how to go about the cultivation of kindness. The self all too readily resorts to the exercise of the will. The will is, after all, the major resource available to the deluded self for powerfully achieving and acquiring whatever it aspires to, and is much encouraged for "getting on" in all walks of life. However, we do not need Dr Freud to remind us of the dangers of top dog trying to kick bottom dog into a state of grace — "You will be kinder next time!" The driven and desiccated moralist to be found in all religious traditions has wrought much damage..

Simone Weil, one of the most insightful mystics of our time, has proposed two legitimate uses for the will in spiritual practice (2). The first is the ethical one of the emergency stop. "STOP! Just don't do it! You know what will happen if you do...". It is only for emergency use, until we have grown ethical personalities, beyond ethical behaviours. The second use of the will is to sustain spiritual practice, which entails for most of us travelling a long and often hard road. However, even here let us be mindful of the middle way and the Buddha's rejection of extreme ascetic practices. The gateless gate in fact lies open, and *virya* (forceful energy) must be balanced by the easeful patience of *ksanti* (patience).

Behavioural Kindness

We are now ready to consider the next level in the cultivation of kindness.

In most Buddhist traditions the *metta-bhavana* practice of loving-kindness meditation is the best known response to the question of how can I be kind? Basically the meditator wishes happiness, well-being and freedom from pain and suffering (or something similar) firstly to his or her self, secondly to a loved one, thirdly to someone for whom their feelings are neutral, and fourthly towards a person for whom they experience enmity. For "wish" the words "may be" or similar expressions are found; the choice is important, to avoid connotations which might encourage the willing of feelings of kindness. Many contemporary versions of this meditation are on offer. One of the more sophisticated is that offered by Ezra Bayda, and not the least interesting in that he is a foremost advocate of the increasingly popular practice of emotional awareness (3). It is significant that Bayda eases the meditator's way in that the fourth and final round is directed not specifically to individuals who are disliked but, more generally, "towards all beings." To make this meditation more accessible "empathy" may be substituted for "kindness". For it is possible to experience empathy toward someone for whom we cannot feel kindness.

In my experience most practitioners do find that this meditation serves to open their hearts and arouse kind feelings and even behaviour towards those with whom they would experience difficulty and resistance. However, I believe a significant minority find resistance to the meditation itself, where it comes to wishing love and kindness to those they dislike — including themselves. And some claim an aversion to what they see as a roundabout willing of inauthentic emotions, such as Cordelia experienced when urged to voice her love for her father. A skilful teacher can turn this to advantage by encouraging the student to go more deeply into this resistance, in other words, to turn the *metta* meditation from a *via positiva* into the more profound *via negativa* which is surely the foundation of Dharma practice. Thus, as I shall argue below, our unkindnesses become our most precious resource in the cultivation of a truly kind personality. The relationship, in this practice context, of *via negativa* and *via positiva* in Buddhism is a fascinating one which merits fuller exploration.

We know from neuroscience and related therapies that the repetition of specific feelings can strengthen the neural pathways and lead to those emotions becoming sufficiently embedded as to change behaviour. At this level loving-kindness meditations undoubtedly "work". They are welcome and valuable in that they offer many people a ready practice enabling them to behave with greater kindness in their lives — which is no small achievement. I would, however, offer two reservations.

First, in view of the desire to be kind of this needy self, there is surely a strong temptation to call up some degree of will in wishing loving kindness. And, as we have seen, the exercise of the will in spiritual practice is to be treated with great circumspection.

Secondly — and more important — there is the danger of spiritual by-passing. That is to say, satisfied with the behavioural effects of loving-kindness meditation, we may fail to pursue more deeply our enquiry into the origins of our inclination to unkindness.

Going Deeper: Wise Kindness

We become profoundly kind not through some impatient, ready-fix grafting of kind behaviour onto our existing personality. A kindness for all seasons is only possible through the patient cultivation of a kind personality. It is the spontaneous kindness of that authentic self to which I briefly referred earlier in this paper.

Wise kindness is distinguished not least by its discriminating clarity. So often we find ourselves involved in situations which move us to speak out or act with what we suppose to be kindness. However we may, unaware, be moved primarily out of a needy anxiety to be kind and to be seen to be kind. Our self-centred view of the situation may blind us to a more realistic appreciation of it. In Zen this is called grandmotherly kindness. Contrariwise, to the extent we have been freed from a self-serving perception, we may discover that we may have to be what appears to be harsh in order in fact to be truly compassionate and helpful. As that Chan classic, *XinXinMing* has it, "When you are not attached to anything, all things are seen as they are".

I shall never forget the graphic accounts given by my first teacher, Ven. Myokyo-ni (then Irmgard Schloegl) of her experiences as a youthful alpinist. Once, on a narrow icy ridge one of the roped-up party panicked and threatened to drag all of them to their deaths. Being "cruel to be kind", the guide had the presence of mind to bring him to his senses by striking him across the face and screaming at him. Less dramatic incidents challenge all of us, when a friend trapped in a difficult personal situation seeks our advice. Fearful of losing a friendship and anxious to display our kindness, do we consolingly support him or her, and even aid and abet what they propose to do, however foolish it privately seems to us? Or, as a true friend, do we tell them some unwelcome home truths, and as a more detached observer, suggest an alternative course of action? It seems to me that where our cultivation of kindness has stopped at the behavioural level we may lack the discriminating wisdom to be truly kind. Moreover if we have cultivated sufficient wisdom, and the equanimity which goes with it, we shall not be afraid of misunderstanding the situation and intervening in a way which turns out to be unhelpful and misleading.

In cultivating, through a deepening emotional awareness, a wise and compassionate personality which can be no other than kind, we shall need wholeheartedly to accept the involuntary unkindnesses to which we fall prey. Like the other discomfitures (and worse) which life inflicts upon the self, we must learn to open ourselves positively, intimately and physically to our unkindness. And no less to the guilt, self-blame which being unkind makes us feel. "May all sorrows ripen in me", proclaims Shanti Deva. In a well-known poem the Sufi sage Rumi urges us to welcome even the ugly and unwelcome guests who turn up on our doorstep, of which our various unkindnesses are surely among the nastiest. (For the poem, see "Talk Seven" in this series.)

This hugely challenging *via negativa* is central to all Buddhist and other spiritual traditions, and I have described it more fully in "Talk Seven: The Practice of Emotional Awareness". Below I offer a reminder and checklist of the different facets of this practice. It is an adaptation of the acronym RAIN. favoured by some mindfulness teachers.

RECOGNITION: Blinded by the strong emotions evoked by some discomfiture of our self we need to recognise explicitly how we feel, even so far as labelling, e.g. "hurt".

ACCEPTANCE: This refers to the heartfelt and positive acceptance of the discomfitures, great and small, which life inflicts upon the self. This is opposite to how we customarily react, and requires a radical turnabout in our attitudes. Acceptance of how things are — their suchness — is fundamental to Buddhist practice, and ultimately an empowerment. It liberates us from the endless conflict between wanting this and rejecting that, which causes so much suffering in our lives.

INVESTIGATION is something of a misnomer. What is required is a profound, intimate and embodied emotional awareness of the painful afflictions in our lives as our fundamental practice, on and — especially — off the cushion. See the papers referred to above.

NON-IDENTIFICATION: This means not taking your feelings so personally; leaving some space around them. That is to say, do not believe all the stories you tell yourself about yourself. Recall the life-long and unwinnable lawsuit which the self conducts against the impermanence and insubstantiality of reality. This creates a distorted and deluded sense of "self". Can we truly believe that is our authentic self?

Gold out of Straw: How to Spin Kindness out of Enmity

Enmity encompasses not only unkindness but ill-will, rancour, hostility, envy, bitterness, resentment, animosity and much other mind-disturbing, guilt-inducing stuff. We may feel it in ourselves, or may be on the receiving end of it, or both. We may feel it towards a parent, child or spouse, towards a co-worker, or towards a public figure. Enmity can give Buddhists a lot of trouble. In many instances our enmity may make us feel doubt, regret, guilt or even pain, especially when someone close to us is involved. At work it may add a disagreeable complication to the everyday demands of the job. And a sense of outrage about the public figures we love to hate does little for our peace of mind. It is also likely to get in the way of a more objective understanding of what they are up to and hence of doing something effective about it.

One response is that we may try to deny our feelings, or feel guilty about them. We may even develop a corrosive enmity against our own selves, because we don't feel as a good self should feel.

The difficulty with enmity is that in many cases there may be very evident grounds for it, whether it be felt by oneself or directed at another. We may be trapped in strong feelings of the injustice done to us, of the unreasonableness of another person. Surely we have some right to feel enmity towards them? Why not give them what they deserve, in a bloody good row, a thorough humiliation, a well-merited sacking, or even a bloody good revolution? And sometimes the sheer force of righteous outrage may appear to flatten the other party and resolve the problem.

Nonetheless, badly hurting with our violence of word or deed a person, or a social class or movement, or a nation, or the natural environment, commonly has a price, paid over the years, poisoning perpetrator and victim alike. There is more than pious homily in the warning in the *Dhammapada* that "Hate is not conquered by hate; hate is conquered by love. This is the eternal law." The twentieth century has the appalling example of the so-called 1914-1945 "war". The Treaty of Versailles that concluded the First World War so humiliated and punished the Germans as to lead directly to the even more destructive Second World War. Usually, whether on the public or personal level, there is no outright victor and only a deepening polarisation, as in the long running enmities of Northern Ireland. And, on the personal level, the unforgiving rancour of divorcing parents can blight several childhoods late into life.

There is a third response to enmity, beyond either denial, guilt or letting it rip. For Buddhists the golden rule is always first to look within, to be scrupulously self-aware. For the present, forget the other. The feelings we experience are our feelings, not theirs. It is our problem (whoever else's it also is), something that we are carrying around with us and which is disturbing us. Just to get to this point of turning the question round may itself bring some relief.

We do not respond to others as if we were dispassionate reflecting mirrors. We respond as precarious, needy beings, struggling in the world to affirm some reassuring sense of self-identity. It is this that characteristically drives our feelings, perceptions and behaviours, and, largely unbeknown, distorts our mirror view of others.

In this connection the Buddha likened our discomfiture to being struck by two arrows when we felt we had been struck by only one. The first arrow is the objective ground for our enmity – the incident, the alleged injury or whatever. The second is how we experience the blow – what it feels like for us. To be aware of this distinction is a vital step in the development of the practice of emotional awareness (4)

Sometimes enmity may arise on the merest pretext. Probably most of us carry around with us in one pocket or another at least a bit of enmity ready for use. After all, surely someone or something must somehow be responsible for the mess? The perpetrators of endemic, low level enmity may be largely unaware of their acerbic manner, their abrasive style, their waspishness. Some books do have a quarrelsome smell about them. I recall a letter to the editor of one of the more fundamentalist ecological magazines. The reader complained that "though in complete agreement with the substance of what you say, there is a spirit of aggression emanating from the pages that makes me recoil from it. I can understand this – there is good reason for anger; the anger appears to have curdled, however, and become vengeful and spite ridden."

The most difficult and important stage in dissolving the experience of enmity lies in cultivating a level of awareness in which we are able to open ourselves clearly, intimately and profoundly into the bare acceptance of that experience. Such emotional honesty can appear hurtful and threatening to our self-esteem, to our very sense of self. We therefore need to be no less aware of our characteristic evasions – fixating on the injury done to us, projecting our indignation on the perpetrator, trying to rationalise our emotional discomfort away (or just denying it altogether), beating ourselves up with guilt, and so on.

As we learn to become intimate and accepting of our own feelings of enmity they begin to release their grip on us. We begin to view the objects of our enmity in their own light, as it were, rather than in ours. George Orwell warned that "one cannot get away from one's subjective feelings, but at least one can get to know what they are and make allowances for them," so as to avoid falling into "a sort of masturbation fantasy in which the world of facts hardly matters" (5).

At this point it will be helpful to reflect as calmly as possible on what actually may have happened. We may then perceive that, for example, a criticism someone made of us was in fact reasonable and well-founded, but that it was made by someone whom we believe dislikes us, and was delivered in a disagreeable manner. So we may then dismiss the criticism as "mere carping" coming from someone whom we could not expect to treat us fairly. We may feel belittled by them or even treated unjustly. In short, we then experience some enmity towards that person.

Accepting our feelings just as they are, we not only start to accept the other (with their enmity) just as they are, but also start to see more clearly the overall situation in which the mutual enmity occurs. The problem then appears more as a situation to be resolved than another person or group to be corrected or punished or defeated. This revelation is commonly accompanied by a release of tension. Once we get the knack of this practice a new lightness of being is possible. For example, the divorcee may abandon with some relief his or her stressful and futile hectoring that the former spouse should change (and perhaps gives up for the present even trying to forgive them). He or she is freed to getting down to negotiating a working partnership in the interests of the children.

Whether at the public or personal levels, none of the foregoing implies any endorsement or acceptance of wrongdoing or injustice. Instead it is about a shift in perception which empowers us to respond to the situation with a new clarity. Freed of what Orwell called "subjective contamination" we are in a much better position to achieve a satisfactory resolution. Mahatma Gandhi, in his use of creative non-violence, was very clear about this. He was always adamant that there should be no compromise on fundamental, reasonable and minimum demands for redress. To the extent that the adversary refused to meet such demands the struggle should resolutely be sustained. But it should no less be a struggle to deepen the adversary's awareness of the suffering and injustice that is being perpetuated, and to do so through mutual respect, genuine communication, and some recognition of common interest.

A willingness to enter into authentic dialogue and a tireless search for an optimal resolution of the problem is the mark of the dissolution of enmity, in at least one party. Where there is a raging confrontation the prospect of constructive dialogue is unwelcome, as a threat to the seamless righteousness with which one or both sides identify. Through such dialogue a constructive and mutually beneficial reconciliation is possible, as in the historic achievement of Nelson Mandela and F.W. de Klerk in South Africa, underpinned by the subsequent Truth and Reconciliation Commission.

Thus, through awareness and acceptance enmity can be dissolved and reconciliation achieved. Beaming loving-kindness (*metta*) to the next crooked politician we hear posturing on the *Today* programme may take longer. However, reconciliation does provide favourable conditions for the arising of loving-kindness and compassion, though best at first to people we can get to know well. And when our awareness practice makes us familiar and accepting of our own frailties, and we come to love ourselves, our hearts are opened more readily to accepting in fellow-feeling the frailties of others.

However, I believe the two most important breakthroughs are when we can distinguish the arrow of affliction from the arrow of experiencing that affliction, and when we can take full responsibility ourselves for the way in which we experience enmity, regardless of the alleged culpability of whoever we may hold responsible. This is nicely illustrated by a parable of the Daoist sage Chuang-Tzu. Rowing across a river our passage may be impeded by empty boats that have got adrift. These we push aside without concern. However, if there are people in the boats, although the problem is the same, we get angry and shout at them for wilfully obstructing us (6).

The above is primarily about the inner work of dissolving personal enmity. In group situations it can be combined with one or more of the many conflict resolution and interpersonal skills strategies and methods that are available. One which works well with what is proposed here is Marshall Rosenberg's Nonviolent Communication (www.cnvc.org).

A postscript on Societal Kindness

For routine public unkindness we need look no further than much of the UK press. It exploits not only greed but also the existential rancour, resentment and negativity exploited by many politicians as in, for example, their populist scapegoating of asylum seekers, "scroungers" and the like. ("After all, someone must be to blame for my unhappiness!") Unkindness does seem to be rife in many areas of public life. (including the heedlessly speedy interactive web). True, a certain "kindness" (often edged with a crowd-catching sentimentality) may be found in the pronouncements of many of the high and mighty. Chekhov was rightly suspicious of such wholesale trade in benevolence, and preferred the retail sort, where hypocrisy is more easily detected.

These many kinds of nastiness out in the public realm have the same gutsy, gratifying feel which most of us find all too familiar in our own outbursts and resentments. The same "fires" of rancour and greed which the Buddha identified in individual lives can be identified and sensationally supercharged in the driven follies of institutions and nations, movements and ideologies on the "butcher's block of history", as Hegel called it. However we define "unkindness" it can hardly be extended to fit, say, the ethnic cleansing of hundreds of thousands of people. We are here moving beyond the scope of this paper and into the discourse of a socially engaged Buddhism which has now become an accepted facet of Dharma. In my book *The New Social Face of Buddhism* (Wisdom, 2003) I have tried to get to the heart of it, and David Loy (among many others) has written wisely and extensively on the same subject, most notably in his *Money, Sex, War and Karma* (Wisdom, 2008). And for the inner work, the personal practice, I would particularly commend Donald Rothberg's *The Engaged Spiritual Life: A Buddhist Approach to Transforming the World* (Beacon Press, 2007).

Nonetheless, if we keep the use of the word within bounds, how to be kind at the public level is as legitimate a call upon us as in our face-to-face lives. And if those closer to us — in need of our help voluntarily or professionally — call more urgently for our time and energy, then so be it, without guilt or blame. The inner work of emotional awareness remains the same, where, in both our kindness and unkindness, we are ripened to become deeply kind people working unreservedly for a kinder world.

(1) David R. Loy *The World is Made of Stories* (Wisdom, 2010, pp64-65).

(2) Simone Weil *Waiting on God.*(Routledge & Kegan Paul, 1979).

(3) Ezra Bayda *Being Zen: Bringing Meditation to Life*(Shambhala, 2003, pp123-128).

(4) The parable of the two arrows will be found in the *Samyutta-nikaya*, xxxvi.6 (the *Sallatha Sutta*).

(5) *George Orwell The Collected Essays, Journalism and Letters* (eds. Sonia Orwell and Ian Angus) (Harcourt Brace Jovanovich, 1968. v3. pp293-299).

(6) Thomas Merton quotes the river crossing parable in his *Way of Chuang-Tzu*, Unwin Books, 1970, p114.

Suchness and This vs. That — Dogen for Beginners

This is a personal presentation of what is to me the essential Eihei Dogen. It is based on half a lifetime of Chan/Zen practice and many years of teaching the practice in a variety of short retreats for both beginners and experienced practitioners. I hope that Dogen beginners may find it of some help in understanding this notoriously challenging thinker and greatest of Zen teachers, who died in 1253.

Duality refers simply to how we make sense of the everyday experience in which we distinguish one thing or quality as different from another to which it is related. Nonduality is the perception of both as a single, undivided holistic experience, termed "suchness" ("thusness") or *tathata*. For example, sometimes we may experience the attractive features of another's personality, but may also refer to some less attractive features. At other times we may simply experience the same personality as a whole, without making such distinctions. Very different is dualism — delusive duality. Here the this versus that distinction is driven by our existential neediness to fortify the fragile self by identifying with whatever strengthens that sense of identity and rejecting and negating whatever appears to deny or threaten it,

"Enlightenment" is a term I have tried to avoid, because of its several possible meanings. For the (more or less) enlightened state I prefer "wisdom". "Suchness"(or "thusness") I use as a comparatively self-explanatory term which embraces both aspects of reality — the relative existence of things and the emptiness of the absolute existence of separate things — "empty" because inconceivable except in terms of their relationship, their duality (their "form"). As Thomas Cleary observes "thusness itself alludes to the simultaneous realisation of emptiness and existence, experiencing directly and openly ...seeing everything as being simply 'thus' ". (*Shobogenzo: Zen Essays by Dogen*. University of Hawaii Press, 1986, p36). The orientation of this paper is that of my own teaching, as set out in my website www.kenjoneszen.com, and is necessary here to provide a context for the relevant Dogen teachings. Much neglected by scholars and, I believe, the summation of his teaching, is what has been called Dogen's "participatory Buddhism" (including social engagement). I have treated this in a separate paper entitled *Zen Master Dogen's Active Compassion*, and it can be found on my website.

Translations of Dogen can vary so greatly as to amount to variant interpretations of his meaning. Books I have found particularly helpful are *Eihei Dogen: Mystical Realist* (Wisdom, 2004) and the shorter *Dogen on Meditation and Thinking* (State University of New York Press, 2007), both by Hee-Jin Kim. Another is John Cleary's *Rational Zen: The Mind of Dogen Zenji* (Shambhala, 1992).

However, I usually refer Dogen beginners to one or, better still, both of the following two short selections: In his *Shobogenzo: Zen Essays by Dogen* Thomas Cleary provides not only translations of these and others, but helpful introductions to each. See also the similar selection of essays and introductions by Norman Waddell and Abe Masao: *The Heart of Dogen's Shobogenzo* (State University of New York, 2002). It is essential not to approach Dogen with the fixed intention of gaining some intellectual meaning from him, and having failed to do so to drop him in frustration and perhaps with a sense of failure. This could come very quickly with the short *Shobogenzo* piece *Ikka Myoju*, which simply proclaims that "all the universe is one bright pearl"! The cultivation of an "understanding" of the concept of suchness can arguably provide a starting point. But let the self retire and leave emotional space for the text itself to do the work, and in its own good time, as with all poetry. Remember that this small self has protected itself with a relatively limited consciousness (Blake's "Mind forg'd manacles"). What Dogen is trying to do is to help the reader greatly to enlarge it. A sense of playful spaciousness is both what is required and what will be repaid. Some experience of koan work can be extremely helpful; indeed, reading Dogen can sometimes feel like facing a succession of koans...

The Existential Tragedy

The typical human condition, cast upon an ocean of impermanence and insubstantiality, is one of profound existential anxiety, of a heartfelt sense of "lack". This is commonly veiled by the degree of success in experiencing whatever imparts a sense of emotional security and a sufficiently strong sense of self-identity, both individual and collective. Especially in modernity, individual achievement and acquisitiveness, as well as the more traditional belongingness, are endeavours for achieving "this". These, however, are precarious, never enough and always threatened by "that" — which is to say everything that threatens to undo the well-fortified sense of self that may have been achieved. In Hubert Benoit's metaphor, this is our long and ultimately unwinnable lawsuit with reality, a lawsuit, incidentally, which is now becoming evident on an historical and global scale. Krishnamurti dramatically expressed it when, in front of an audience, he displayed a gap between the thumb and index finger of one of his hand, proclaiming that all the miseries of the world were to be found in that gap, the gap between the "this" of our existential needy self and the "that" of all the forces that threaten to deprive us of it.

"This" versus "that" is, I believe, the starting point for an understanding of Dogen. The theme that runs through the essays in his great collection the *Shobogenzo* is the unmasking of this delusive dualism, and demonstrating the Great Way of opening to a sense of *duality* which is freed of the self-neediness which drives *dualism*. The distinction between duality and dualism was nicely encapsulated by R H Blyth in his observation that things may be hopeless, but not dispiriting; unjust, but not hateful; beautiful, but not desirable; loathsome but not rejected.

An opening to duality opens the way to *suchness*, which sees the duality of this and that in their oneness, their wholeness. Thus, in the *Xin-xin-ming* (a seventh century foundational scripture of the Chan tradition): "When we stop movement, there is no movement; when we stop rest, there is no rest; these are two names of one thinglessness." For example, as an erstwhile prison chaplain, the convicted inmates I encountered were undoubtedly bad fellows, but when I got to know them better it became clear that each also possessed good attributes. And on deeper acquaintance I was able to perceive the whole man in his suchness, and better able to appreciate how he had come to where he was now.

The Great Way

The practice of the Great Way, the opening of delusion to wisdom, involves a transcendent shift from one kind of consciousness to another. Inevitably elements of our delusive consciousness become unknowingly embodied in the very practice whereby we hope to *achieve* this existential revolution. This perception is experienced in dualistic terms which Dogen was determined, again and again, to uproot. The practice is typically understood in terms of endeavours like learning to use a computer or play tennis. By strenuous application of the will we advance step by step over time to greater levels of competence, with corresponding awards and recognition both by self and others, and hope finally to become acknowledged experts. Thus, in our "law suit with reality" we hope to achieve the stronger self-identity for which we yearn. This can be an insidious and deeply embedded urge. It is the more so when institutionalised, leading sometimes to what Jung called "spiritual inflation" of the ego, with the corruption of spiritual insights, and a "spiritual bypassing" whereby the practice becomes a thing-in-itself beyond the rest of the practitioner's life. He or she is urged on with metaphors like climbing a glass mountain, the whole process attended by some stress and anxiety, and perhaps competition with peers. There is an assumption that eventual failure may result in an awareness of the futility of this scenario and that deeply felt acceptance which is essential in the shift towards wisdom

Deluded beginners understandably see the mastery of the specialised technique of meditation as the key to achievement — in this case of "enlightenment", the achievement of an entirely new self. In the Zen tradition this means *zazen*, which, with Dogen, apparently refers not only to sitting meditation but to mindfulness and reflective practice in other situations. Again and again Dogen emphasises the need to free one's meditation from any trace of gaining or achieving: what is important is sustained practice. "If you wish to practice the way of the Buddhas ... you should expect nothing, seek nothing. Cut off the mind that seeks and do not cherish a desire to gain the fruits of Buddhahood" (*Zuimonki*). In *zazen*, he taught, enlightenment and practice are one and the same., Thus our Buddha nature is already enlightened before we mature sufficiently to open fully to enlightenment (wisdom). In the same vein, Shunryu Suzuki wrote:

> Which is more important: to attain enlightenment, or to attain enlightenment before we attain enlightenment? To make a million dollars or to enjoy your life in your effort, little by little, even though it is impossible to make that million; to be successful or to find meaning in your effort to be successful? If you do not know the

answer you will not even be able to practice *zazen*; if you do know you will have found the true treasure of life" (*Zen Mind, Beginner's Mind*, pp122–123).

He clarifies: "Whether you practice *zazen* or not you have the Buddha nature. Because you have it there is enlightenment in your practice. The point we emphasize is not the stage we attain, but the strong confidence in our original nature and the sincerity of our practice... practice based on any gaining idea is just a repetition of your karma. Forgetting this idea, many late Zen masters have emphasized some stage to be obtained... We do not slight the idea of attaining, but the important thing is this moment, not some day in the future" (*op.cit.*, pp99–101).

I suspect that in sanghas where attainment is emphasised this must diminish the prominence given to our Buddha nature ("Big Mind"), for which I prefer the term "authentic nature"), even though there is a danger of seeing two selves — top dog and bottom dog. The deluded self and the authentic self are, of course, simply manifestations of the same self. The latter is recognizable by its spontaneity as when we are naturally moved by compassion to intervene when, say, we see an animal mistreated. But, of course, our motives tend to be mixed, and not least when we are moved to help, as David Brandon showed so eloquently in his "Zen and the Art of Helping". The needy self loves to feel "good" and "kind" or maybe somehow superior to the one who requires his or her help. And can one say how far one's love for one's nearest and dearest springs from a selfless spontaneity of affection and how far from more calculative motives? At all events the cultivation of a belief that one is, at bottom, wise and compassionate is surely better than a dominant sense of inadequacy and battling one's lawsuit against reality.

Opening to Wisdom and Compassion

For Dogen faith lay in our original sense of being enlightened, in our authentic nature, "Faith is one with the fruit of enlightenment; the fruit of enlightenment is one with faith." (*Gakudo Yojinshu I*, 9). Hee-Jin Kim claims that "Dogen's view of faith in terms of trust, obedience, dependence, surrender, and commitment is clear". (*Eihei Dogen: Mystical Realist*, 271n.). Kim comments further:

> Faith and enlightenment are often regarded as two antithetical ideas, so much so that Zen Buddhism can be mistakenly thought to be exclusively the religion of enlightenment, while faith is an inferior or foreign element, or at best a preliminary step to enlightenment. But in Dogen's thought faith and enlightenment interpenetrated one another, so that without one the other could not be fully meaningful. The inferior status of faith was repudiated once and for all by Dogen; it now became for him the very core of enlightenment" (op.cit. 66).

I recall a distinction which Ken Wilber once made between belief and faith. The former is rational and intellectual. We hear or read the Dharma and conclude that it makes sufficient sense in terms of our own life experience for us to take up the practice. In due course, if all goes well, we "wear out the sandal of samsara". That is to say, we begin to open in profound acceptance to our life as we experience it — things are as they are, in their suchness, and that evasive lawsuit with reality is a futile delusion. We enter the realm of faith, that life is somehow basically okay, and begin to share the wisdom of the mystics, as expressed by T S Eliot in "The Four Quartets":

> All shall be well;
>
> All manner of things shall be well.

Here we begin to enter the realm of wisdom and compassion ("enlightenment) which will ripen henceforth, without any illusion of perfection or arrival. "When you are not attached to anything, all things are as they are", as the *Xin-xin-ming* reiterates. Here is the watershed in spiritual experience where the real practice begins. The self is increasingly at ease with self and others, and increasingly at one with all that is other ("unity consciousness"). Playfulness and a sense of spaciousness — characteristics of Zen — begins to blossom, as an attribute of the Bodhisattvas, of whom it is said that they go down into hell to rescue lost souls as if it were a fairground.

A reading of Dogen implies, in my view, that these shifts are not necessarily characterised by powerful insights, including the celebrated *kensho* of "mind and body dropped off". Except that the shift into faith, whether gradual or sudden, is itself arguably an insight, coming as it does with the force of fact. Shunryu Suzuki was explicit about this: "If you have great faith and great acceptance there is no need to worry about enlightenment. This may come along some time as an optional extra; it doesn't matter." Note that here "enlightenment" is referred to as an insight, and not as a state of mind, which I refer to as "wisdom".

Essays in Dogen's *Shobogenzo* collection helpfully explore the nature of suchness through examples, of which the most readily accessible, in my view, are "Being Time" (*Uji*), "Birth and Death" (*Shoji*), "Flowers in the Sky" (*Kuge*), and "The Scripture of Mountains and Rivers" (*Sansuikyo*), to which might be added "Painting of a Rice Cake". One's penetration of the concepts of suchness, duality and emptiness becomes more problematic when explored at their conceptual limit, for example in Dogen's *Ikka Myoju* ("One Bright Pearl") — "All the universe is one bright pearl".... The difficulty had already been spelt out several centuries earlier in the *XinXinMing* ("On Faith in the Heart"), attributed to Seng-ts'an, the Third Chan

Patriarch, here in the Arthur Waley translation, and surely as near as one might get to conceptualising suchness:

> The infinitely small is as large as the infinitely great, when boundaries and distinctions are forgotten.

> The infinitely large is as small as the infinitely minute, when its outlines are not seen by any eye.

A little playfulness goes a long way here...

Here are two examples which my retreat students appear to find helpful to work with.

First — excluding romantic (and delusive) affairs — recall someone with whom you are, or have been, in love (this invariably encompasses the majority). Then recall what you felt to be their good points, and secondly, what you didn't like about them. Then conjure up feelings of love which subsume both your likes and dislikes. I suggest to them that this suchness offers a ready definition of "love". They then discuss in small groups, each one including those who feel they have been in love. Discussion stimulates and amplifies. It also acknowledge Dogen's emphasis on language, and on thinking and "non-thinking" (see later).

A more accessible exercise in suchness is the example of Dogen's duality of fleeting time and time being. The students are first invited to note the usually wide span of ages in the room, and then to conceive each person as existing "just as they are", regardless of age. This other pole of the duality is itself illustrative also of suchness, in that it subsumes the more ingrained and familiar pole of age. We may be both conscious of another's age but *no less and at the same time* of other impressions they make unconnected with their age. This subsuming of both is the explicit perception of suchness. A similar exercise may be approached through the koan "There is no time; what is memory? "

These examples suggest further explorations and workshops in the application of Dogen's dialectical duality to personal and social relations, at work and elsewhere. Scholars have now for some time been exploring the relevance of Dogen's thought to contemporary philosophy and, latterly, language and literature. I suggest that there is much to be done...

Beyond Quietism: Dogen's Participatory Buddhism

It is possible to stop there and dwell in the contemplative bliss of the wisdom of suchness. However, where self is at one with all that is other (or even just wholeheartedly at ease with self and others), what else is there to do but compassionately and actively to heed the cries of others and the plight of our planet? This bodhisattva "return to the market place" is the summation of the well known Zen series of bull-taming pictures. Dogen, however, would have undoubtedly had his seeker taming the bull also *in the market place* from the start, as proclaimed in the following quotation which opens my separate paper on participatory Buddhism entitled "Zen Master Dogen's Active Compassion" :

> Those who regard worldly affairs as an obstacle to their training do

> not realise that there is nothing such as worldly affairs to be distinguished from the Way (Bendowa — *Wholehearted Practice*).

Thus the opening to wisdom is no less the opening to compassion, into a *participatory* Buddhism, whether of family carer or a self-sacrificing social activist. Dogen's participatory Buddhism is fully discussed in my paper *Zen Master Dogen's Active Compassion*, which can be found on my website www.kenjoneszen.com.

Thinking, Language and Literature

Customarily Zen practitioners are warned to eschew thinking and language, which are understood only in terms of the discriminative dualism which the practice is designed to dissolve. In his pioneering work *Reading Emptiness: Buddhism and Literature* (SUNY, 1999) Jeff Humphries claims that Buddhism, and particularly Zen, "have been deeply corrupted by this misapprehension that texts – language and literature – could not contribute to enlightenment, to the direct apprehension of reality." He denies that either the Buddha or Nagarjuna implied this – and certainly not Dogen.

Most notably in his *Shobogenzo* essay "Picture of a Rice Cake" Dogen refutes the dualist belief that the act of reading, or viewing a picture (or, presumably, listening to music) involves an animated sentient being, with an inherent existence, confronting an inanimate thing. (The Red Queen in Lewis Carroll's *Through the Looking-glass* would have something to say about *that*). A text, a picture, a piece of music, has its own life once its creator has sent it forth, with whatever meaning he or she has sought to endow it. And readers, viewers and listeners will, in turn, attribute their own meanings, and maybe argue about which is "correct".

How often may we read a novel and people our life with its vivid imaginings which, like a dream, may appear more real than the perhaps drear and mundane realities of our own daily life? Noteworthy here is a story, entitled *Sailing Home* (Free Press, 2008), in which Zen Master Norman Fischer uses Homer's *Odyssey* as analogy to help his readers to navigate the pitfalls and perils of their own lives. He writes:

> Somewhere we've developed the misconception that poetry is self-expression, and that meditation is going inward. Actually, poetry has nothing to do with self-expression, it is the way to be free, finally, of self-expression, to go much deeper than that. And

meditation is not a form of thought or reflection, it is a looking at or an awareness of what is there, equally inside and outside, and then it doesn't make sense anymore to mention inside or outside.

The foregoing applies especially to haiku and its related form of haibun (haiku-like prose pieces), which are one of the Zen "ways" (do) of practice, together with martial arts, calligraphy and the like. Haiku confine themselves to concrete images as open metaphors to express meanings, leaving more space than is usual in poetry for readers' imaginations. I have examined this further in my website www.kenjoneszen.com, where I note that the urge of the ego to express itself is the main enemy of the *haijin*.

Further, Zen poetry and prose (and especially Dogen's) may be presented in a nondualistic style which exemplifies Dogen's term "non-thinking", (as opposed dualistic "thinking"), where sunrise occurs at midnight. This opens for us a suchness beyond our accustomed this-and-that which are, no less, mere words. Consider these two examples from *Crow with No Mouth*, being the "versions" by Stephen Berg of the poetry of the fifteenth century Zen Master Ikkyu (Copper Canyon Press, 1989:

This ink painting of wind blowing through the pines

who hears it?

not two not one either

and the unpainted breeze in the ink painting feels cool

Dogen's trinary complex of Thinking, Not-thinking and Non-thinking

At the heart of Dogen's emphasis on dualism, duality and suchness is his clarification of the place of thinking in Zen practice, hence the use of the words "mystical realism" and "rational Zen" in the books by Hee-Jin Kim and Thomas Cleary. Yet Dogen's insistence on the centrality of thinking in *zazen* by no means implies a dismissal of those profound insights variously described as kensho, peak experience, and the ineffable. It is just that he was more concerned with how practitioners might communicate and implement such experiences in terms of language and life in the world.

Arguably Dogen's not-thinking also extends to more modest experiences, as when the mind simply falls still and momentarily goes blank. Thus he writes of *zazen* that "whenever a thought occurs be aware of it, and it will vanish. If you remain for a long period forgetful of objects, you will naturally become unified. This is the essential art of *zazen*" (Carl Bielfeldt *Dogen's Manuals,* p181)that is, non-thinking. This is the "backward step" of turning the light within to observe one's own awareness, the "silent illumination" already described by Chan Master Hongzhi a century earlier. Dogen paraphrased the above quotation by quoting a story about Yaoshan (745-828), who was asked what he thought about when meditating. He replied that he thought of that which doesn't think (that is to say, by "non-thinking"). Asked further about how he did that he replied "beyond thinking" (that is, by "not-thinking").

Non-thinking is thus, as I understand it, the cognitive articulation of suchness, as in, for example, the insight that everything is basically okay — "all things shall be well".

"Thinking" is the duality where there are both things which are and are not well. Non-thinking can only come forth when thinking is suspended by not-thinking. As explained earlier in this paper, (with a quotation from R H Blyth), the thinking of duality is nonetheless essential simply to distinguish one thing from another. The tragedy of the human condition is typically how this duality is corrupted into the fear-driven dualism of a lifestyle of wanting this and rejecting that — an evasion the futility of which is *dukkha* — suffering.

Koans

For Dogen koan practice is the natural accompaniment of "just sitting", and not an opposed practice, as is often supposed. In terms of language, an acceptable response to a koan is the expression in non-thinking to a statement presented as an illogical paradox, that is to say, as "thinking", for example "Nothing matters; everything matters".

The Soto Zen tradition prefers to use koans in terms of our personal experience of the discomfitures and problems of our daily lives, rather than as abstract and decontextualised problems which have a poor transference and application to our everyday lives, and which can therefore lead to spiritual bypassing. Dogen's dictum that, in *zazen*, practice and enlightenment are one could be used as a koan in that it presents a paradox, since, in terms of "thinking", of duality, they are separate, sequential and opposed activities. Since practice leads to enlightenment; how can they be identical?

Traditionally and conventionally koans, as formulated to Westerners by D T Suzuki, are used to by-pass "words and phrases", which are seen only as dualistic thinking from which the practice is intended to free us. Their paradoxical presentation is designed to exasperate and frustrate the practitioner who tackles them head-on, to bankrupt the intellect, and confront him or her with an impasse. The resulting despair and bafflement is designed to break down conventional consciousness and induce the dawning of a transcendent awakening. The paradox of the koan is dissolved into a world of wordless experience — an approach which ignores language through which we transact our lives. Nonetheless, experience of working with koans can be invaluable in weaning us from the either-this-or-that mentality.

The Emotional Climate of Nondualistic Practice

I believe that the emotional climate generated by nondualistic practice, individually and also collectively (in a sangha or on a retreat), differs from that of a practice which tends to emphasize the attainment of higher spiritual states. If we feel we are already intrinsically wise and compassionate, even though we have yet fully to manifest it, then our practice is surely less anxious and stressed, and more playful. Certainly that has been my experience with retreat participants. Again, the great Chan poem "Faith in the Heart" (*Xin-Xin-Ming*) offers the reassurance of living in suchness, as in the following passage (Waley translation):

The Great Way is calm and large hearted;

for it nothing is easy, nothing hard.

small and partial views are uncertain and insecure;

sometimes assertive, sometimes vacillating.

When you are not attached to anything,

all things are as they are.

There follows the following encouraging passage (this time Alan Watts's version):

Follow your nature and accord with the Way;

saunter along and stop worrying;

when your thoughts are tied you spoil what is genuine.

Do not be antagonistic to the world of the senses,

for when you are not, it turns out to be the same as complete awakening.

The wise person does not strive; the ignorant tie themselves up;

If you work on your mind with your mind,

How can you avoid complete confusion?

Likewise, we practice scales on the piano confident that, with persistence, we shall in due course play music. Similarly, we can relax splashing around in the shallow end if confident that one day we shall find ourselves floating. In meditation such attitudes will be more readily engendered if we realise that a striving acquisitiveness is precisely what we wish to let go in the first place.

Instead of a blinkered purposiveness to "batter down the Dharma gates", the relaxed, nondualistic state of mind frees us to open to the deeper mysteries of experience. For while it is true that our everyday mental constructs enable us to impart order and definition to the cosmic chaos of sense experience, we forget that the world as we have defined it at the same time defines us. The puppet master becomes a puppet of the toys he has created. A relaxed experience of our authentic, Buddha nature the better enables us to detach from what are only our mental creations.

At home in our Buddha nature, but doubtless no less aware of our still persistent delusiveness, we open in ready compassion to the misfortunes and stupidities of others. We are the more aware that however deeply we may open to wisdom we never transcend our everyday humanity for something "higher". Thus, Dogen in his opening passage about enlightenment and delusion in the *Genjokoan*, adds the moving remark "Yet in attachment blossoms fall, and in aversion weeds spread." In his writing the compassionate suchness that embraces all contrasts, all dualities, shines forth again and again. In the same essay there is this wonderful declaration of Zen humanism (which also provides an excellent definition of suchness), rendered as follows by some inspired translator:

> Every creature covers the ground it stands on, no more nor no less, it never fall short of its completeness.

Finally, here are two of Dogen's poems, as translated by Steven Heine in his "Zen Poetry of Dogen" (Tuttle, 1997):

The true person is

Not anyone in particular;

But, like the deep blue colour

Of the limitless sky,

Is everyone, everywhere in the world.

The unspoilt colours of a late summer night,

The wind howling through the lofty pines —

The feel of autumn approaching:

The swaying bamboos keep resonating,

And shedding tears of dew at dawn;

Only those who exert themselves fully

Will attain the Way.

But even if you abandon all for the ancient path of meditation

You can never forget the meaning of sadness.

Ageing: the Great Adventure
A Buddhist Guide

1 – The Art of Ageing

It was the shock of witnessing sickness, old age and death at first hand that moved the youthful Prince Siddhartha Gautama, the future Buddha, to search for a way out of suffering. Those of us who are no longer young are faced with the same challenge more directly. How can we best respond to it?

Ageing is the supreme challenge of our life. Physically we begin to deteriorate. Socially we may now find ourselves discounted and patronised in various subtle and not so subtle ways. Ageism is the last and most difficult of the discriminations to be rooted out. These physical and social discomfitures combine to threaten and undermine our self-image and how we value ourselves. Commonly old age is viewed as a time when the best of life is behind us. What remains is to enjoy the "compensations" of old age, and even these are customarily presented in a sentimental and patronising light.

I offer here a very different perspective, a Buddhist perspective, together with some practical proposals about how to embody it. Ageing can be the culminating adventure of our lives, up to which the earlier years may be seen as a *preparation*. I do not refer here to the promise of perpetual youth peddled by golden oldie consumerism. That is more evasion than adventure. The adventure of ageing is nothing less than opportunity to transcend the self which has lived its life up to now, and hence to transcend the decrepitude and death of that self. At its simplest that grand word "transcendence" is about being totally at ease with ourselves, and hence at ease with others. Freed from self preoccupations and anxieties we can wholeheartedly serve others.

The essence of an adventure, however, is that it is scary and unpredictable, a venture into the unknown which demands courage and risking ourselves. The more we resort to safety-nets, diversions and evasions the less of an adventure it becomes. We sell ourselves short.

Moreover, an adventure requires training, skill and practice. So if we are to make an art of growing old and dying we need a practice, a way of cultivation, not as a part-time hobby, but with all our heart all our time. What I shall offer here is a number of perspectives and practices which readers can adapt to their own situations and needs. They will be around four themes: ageing, physical embodiment, dying, and celebration.

Making a Start

"Suffering I teach, and the way out of suffering", proclaimed the Buddha. Here "suffering" does not mean pain but the profound discomfiture which we experience when all our attempts to remedy or evade pain prove futile. Our suffering presents us with a powerful incentive to undertake a practice in which we learn to work intimately with the suffering and thereby transform it or at the least make it more manageable.

So the first task of each of us is to identify and define what it is about ageing that particularly discomfits and frustrates us. Where is the shoe pinching? Indeed we may be able to identify and work with two or three such discomfitures.

Note that what we have to work with is not the *cause* of our discomfiture (that is, the pain itself) but how we *experience* it (that is, our sense of discomfiture) — not what is afflicting us out there, but what it feels like in here, in the mind. The Buddha explained this distinction between pain and suffering from pain as follows:

When afflicted with a feeling of pain those who lack inner awareness sorrow, grieve and lament, beating their breasts and becoming distraught. So they feel two pains, physical and mental. It is just like being shot with an arrow, and right afterwards being shot with a second one, so that they feel two arrows.

Some people find it difficult to make this distinction, but to be able to do so is a first big step towards overcoming suffering. Thus we may be afflicted by the pain of arthritis, plus the painful fact of not being able to manage on a reduced income. Secondly, we need to clarify consciousness of how each of these afflictions upsets us. How this is to be done will be explained shortly. But it is noteworthy that different people may experience much the same affliction in very different ways. Some make light of what others find deeply depressing.

External fixes

In our contemporary culture a great many afflictions can be remedied or alleviated by some external fix. Medication can control arthritic pain. State welfare benefits can alleviate financial distress. Certainly such remedies should be explored and applied as needs be.

Those of us who are financially comfortable and live in prosperous high tech cultures have access to so many external fixes that we tend to develop a "fix it" mentality. We become totally dependent on external solutions and feel particularly frightened and vulnerable when these are not available or do not work any longer. This contrasts with more traditional cultures where greater psycho-spiritual and cultural resources have been developed to enable people to *experience* affliction less painfully in the substantial absence of technical and social fixes. However, with ageing, medical interventions and favourable social conditions can be only of limited value in the face of our mortality and the inevitable deterioration of our bodies. It is this that makes the experience of ageing particularly challenging.

It is our self-identity that is challenged. This vulnerable and transient sense of self needs to affirm itself, to feel secure, by holding on to whatever it can, getting enough of what it wants and avoiding enough of what it doesn't want. For a variety of reasons this tends to become more difficult with ageing, and there is commonly a growing sense of powerlessness and loss of control over our lives. This exposes the root fear, the sense of *lack*, that lies at the heart of the human condition but which in earlier years we are better placed to keep covered up.

Threats to the Ageing Self

There are two intertwined strategies by which we struggle to sustain our sense of self in the course of our lives. They are belongingness-identity (of gender, nationality and so on) and strongly standing out as a unique individual who makes his or her mark. Both of these identity-creating strategies are threatened by ageing.

On the day I retired from my institutional career, cleared my desk, and handed in my ID card, I recall wandering about disconsolately amidst the rush of purposive commuters, who knew where they were going that day, and probably for several years to come. "Retired" and "O.A.P." are back-number identities which imply a kind of belongingness we may be reluctant to embrace. Behind the social invisibility of old age there is much alienation and loneliness. This includes alienation from our contemporary speedy, clever youth culture, which can become increasingly strange with each passing decade. The aged tend to become strangers in their own land.

Ours is an up-front culture of individualism with attitude. Get a life! In a culture which places a high value on independence, standing up and standing out, physical and financial dependence can induce feelings of failure and inadequacy.

In the area of gender and sexuality to be a "real man" or a "real woman" is commonly important in sustaining a strong self-identity. Here again old age can diminish self-regard. Men's sexual drive is lost or diminished; women are said to lose their looks.

Responses to Ageing — Keeping Young

It is just possible for a few to avoid both the tribulations and the challenges of ageing, and never really to grow old at all. These are commonly robust, healthy and well-to-do extraverts who manage to keep reinventing their youthful selves, always on the go. Then one day they go out like a light, perhaps in their sleep, perhaps from a heart attack. Still as busy and self-fulfilled as ever they crash into the buffers and are gone.

In our culture this is widely considered the best possible way to go. And indeed such a life may be envied by those for whom ageing is a wretched decline. Of all the geriatric evasion strategies it is deservedly the most popular, though not one that can always be chosen at will. But is there not something supremely important which this eternal-youth-and-into-the-buffers school may be missing?

Many of those who strive to keep young find that being actively involved in service to others helps them to do this. Thus life continues to appear meaningful and they have the status of the helper who assists the needy. But for people of any age, helping others can be a major distraction from truly seeking to help ourselves. True, the aged have many opportunities to be of service to others in ways not possible when younger. However, what that service really *means* depends on motivation. How far are we really serving ourselves and how far are we selflessly serving others? Only the cultivation of scrupulously honest insight can give a clear answer. For if we are predominantly serving our selves then the quality of our service is likely to be flawed. This is a difficult and delicate matter. We should certainly not be deterred from helping others if they are in need and we feel we can be of assistance. It is by the actual experience of helping that we have an opportunity to observe what underlying motivations are at work. And certainly if we are helping older people one of the most valuable services we can offer is to become an example of how to age in an inspiring and creative way ourselves.

Some Negative Responses to Ageing

Jung observed that "many old people prefer to be hypochondriacs, niggards, pedants, applauders of the past or else eternal adolescents. – all lamentable substitutes for the illumination of the self."

In response to the multiple discomfitures of ageing, our personality and behaviour may be deformed, though we may remain unaware of the extent to which we have changed. We may become curmudgeonly, grudging and cantankerous, full of bile against the world for all we have lost. Why me? From there it is an easy slide into self-pity and then into depression and then into withdrawal and denial – seemingly bereft of all emotion. Our immune system weakens and we become an easy prey to illness.

A different response is to play the Uncle Tom role. We reinvent ourselves as old fogies (which is at least some kind of distinctive identity) or, better still, we cosy up to being patronised as jolly old birds and amiable codgers.

Another kind of evasion is that of the fusspot, struggling desperately to keep everything in place. We become anxious and obsessive about more and more petty details. It is as if our larger concerns had now escaped us (or we had managed to forget them) and hence control over what remains to us becomes increasingly important. And yet for others growing old brings the opposite — an enlargement of all our sensibilities.

And, finally, the Existential Option

Advancing age makes it more and more difficult for us to feel in full control of our lives. It loosens our grip on many of our attachments. It helps us to let go of clinging. For the first time we may sense the full human potential that lies beyond this small, obsessed self.

And so the third kind of response is to undertake a transformation of the experience of ageing. There are some people who seem able to do this quite naturally and effortlessly. But the meditative practice of "bare awareness" (or "mindfulness") through which it can be achieved is available to all of us.

A start has been made already here with the identification of each of our own most acutely felt discomfitures of ageing. Discomfiture refers here to the painful experience of some external affliction, including bodily afflictions.

Awareness practice is learning to open up to powerful emotions without either letting them discharge themselves (as anger or self-pity, for example), or suppressing them (perhaps by trying to rationalize them or otherwise get them under control). This, incidentally, is not to deny that anger may be a healthy response to some injustice out there — but when angry we can often sense how much is in fact coming from some gutsy ego frustration. This middle way of creative containment is not easy to describe, and harder still to do. It requires a lot of personal experimentation.

John Welwood, a transpersonal psychologist, writes of "befriending emotion" which, "by neither suppressing emotions nor exploring the meaning in them, teaches us a way to feel their naked aliveness and contain their energy." Some further explanation from teachers in different Buddhist traditions may help to get the measure of awareness practice. In the Theravada Buddhist tradition, Nyanaponika Mahathera writes that "by the methodical application of Bare Attention ... all the latent powers of a non-coercive approach will gradually unfold themselves with their beneficial results and their wide and unexpected implications." "Let yourself be in the emotion", wrote the Tibetan Buddhist teacher Chögyam Trungpa. "Go through it, give in to it, experience it... Then the most powerful energies become absolutely workable rather than taking you over, because there is nothing to take over if you are not putting up any resistance." Zen philosopher Hubert Benoit warns as follows: "If a humiliating circumstance turns up, offering me a marvellous chance of initiation, at once my imagination strives to conjure what appears to me to be in danger... It does everything to restore me to that habitual state of satisfied arrogance in which I find a transitory respite, but also the certainty of further distress. In short, I constantly defend myself against that which offers to save me; I fight foot by foot to defend the very source of my unhappiness! "

Thus, in ageing, we seek to open in stark awareness to one or more of the particular discomfitures — hurts, anxiety, unease — which we have identified, working for a period of time with each if there are more than one. These feelings are threatening when we try to look them straight in the face. It is like spilling cold water on a hot stove: the bubbles run in all directions and turn to steam. Anything to escape! For this reason it is best to begin with whatever might be our favourite *evasions* of a specific discomfiture. We can begin by examining possible evasion in terms of lifestyle, as described earlier, like the escape into busyness or into fussy and petty preoccupations.

Next we can move in closer and try to get a taste of the inner, psychological evasions that lie beneath what I have called lifestyle evasions. For example, Elizabeth Kübler Ross identified a sequence of successive attitudes to death and dying as denial, anger, bargaining, depression, and finally acceptance.

We each have our favourite evasions when blocked, frustrated or frightened by some circumstance that threatens our control over our lives. In my experience, strongly masculine personalities often fixate on "my problem out there" and may find it very difficult to get in touch with "how it feels in here". Another first line of defence is denial ("I'm not really ill at all!"). Or we may try to rationalise and intellectualise painful feelings (like kidding ourselves we are not really in denial, or burying ourselves − thanks to the internet! − in study and discussion of the minutiae of our illness). Or, again, anger and frustration may be projected onto others or the world in general ("Young people today...."). Even feeling guilty is evasive, in that by punishing *ourselves* we do retain a perverse kind of control. The same can be said of self-pity, often a final resort. Here we are getting down to very basic emotions, stripping away successive self-protecting layers. Anger itself, for example, is an evasion which protects us from what we eventually discover lies beneath it and fires it up − root fear.

Always this practice is about deepening our physical awareness of how affliction feels. What are its physical sensations? Its colour? The taste of it? Getting in touch will be easiest in sitting meditation, when the surface of the mind has become still and the deeper feelings can be observed.

When the root fear in which our evasions originate does itself become transparent we are left only with the emptiness of the self-seeking self. The self just gives up trying to sustain its illusions (sometimes in a state of extreme despair) and is freed at last into acceptance of the "suchness" of things, of "just how it is", "just how we are". Reality appears without our need to colour and shape it, to make pictures, and hence we become more open to other people's realities. Indeed, it has always been there, trying to break through to us, but obscured by the clouds of self-protectiveness. There is here a sense of liberative joy, of gratitude, freed of the constant strain of trying to make our condition as we vainly desire it to be. Note that "acceptance" here signifies a positive liberation instead of the grudging putting up with things that the word might otherwise suggest.

Similarly the "empowerment" we experience is not a self-empowerment, but the empowerment of a universal energy that floods in when we give up our futile attempts at self-empowerment. When all our evasions become transparent they lose their compulsive power. We see more clearly how to respond to our problems, which now appear more open and manageable. And if there is little we can do about our decrepitude and death in a few years time, in that deep hearted acceptance lies liberation.

Stacking firewood

this winter evening

how simple death seems

Freed of self-preoccupation we are freed wholly to respond to others' needs. The wisdom of bare awareness thus manifests itself as compassion in the world. Laughter and tears mingle when we become aware of the tragi-comedy of our unavailing struggle to be free of this or that without being able to see that struggle as itself the greatest of our problems.

This, then, is how we can transcend ageing as it is conventionally experienced. And it is with ageing that this practice achieves its greatest potential, when all the customary evasions to which we may have become habituated in earlier years begin to wear thin and we are obliged truly to confront our human condition.

2 — Embodying our Age

Shaving mirror

an ancient man surprised

stares back

And the full length mirror may be even more nakedly discomfiting. Who is this staring back at us? This seemingly unchanging *me* is confronted by this thing I own as "my body". And yet how can it be no more than something dangling at the end of my mind? For as this body deteriorates, its pains multiply, disturbing the "I" who once took my body very much for granted.

Women in particular may begin to feel more at home in their bodies only with the onset of ageing. There are various possible reasons for this, such as the alienation experienced by women traditionally presented as objects of desire, and in some cultures, repressive attitudes to sex and the body.

For the most part, however, our youthful embodiment tends to be narcissistic, stimulated by a commercialised culture of physical improvement, youthful appearance, and obsessional sex. With ageing we may begin to experience embarrassment with our bodies and even revulsion. A once-prized exhibit becomes a liability.

Most religious traditions have tended to revile the body. The concern has been to discourage any inclination to identify with our sensuous flesh — and even more so with somebody else's. Women especially have been seen as (for men) dangerously embodied creatures and a threat to ascetic rectitude.

So far I have supposed a dualistic understanding of mind versus a "separate" body, a split mind/body person. Krishnamurti once observed that all the miseries of the world were to be found in even the smallest gap between *this* and *other*, in other words, in dualistic perceptions. Here the challenge of old age is for the self to embody itself, for mind and body to be experienced as one.

Such an embodiment can occur spontaneously when the self-consciousness of body and mind are lost in some absorbingly creative task, in athletic and sporting skills, in making love, and so on. Pairing meditation with hatha yoga makes for a particularly valuable embodiment practice. And the practice of bare awareness as previously described is, of course, also a healing embodiment, working with the physicality of emotion, and particularly with physical pain. This is a large subject in itself, but Stephen Levine's book *Who Dies?* has a particularly valuable chapter on working with pain.

As our ageing body accumulates aches and pains these become not a distraction from cultivating meditative awareness but an ally, strongly holding our attention and keeping us earthed. In the mind's meditative experience of the body, body and mind become the one *presence* which is no longer an awareness of any *thing*. This in its purest form is an awakening from life's dream.

3 — Ageing into Dying and Death

Buddhist writer Larry Rosenberg maintains that "we're not really afraid of dying — we're afraid of the *idea* of dying". The discussion of ideas about dying has become quite fashionable — though they are not usually recognised as no more than ideas. The *Tibetan Book of the Dead* and its famous variant, Sogyal Rinpoche's *Tibetan Book of Living and Dying*, have become bestsellers. At any public meeting on Buddhism you can be sure of at least one question about rebirth.

In meditative enquiry it is important to distinguish between ideas and personal experience. Buddhist ideas about death are an expression of the experience of highly evolved *yoginis*, raised in or living in traditional spiritually saturated cultures.

Such ideas can sustain faith. They are also valuable in that they may contain specific meditation and visualisation instructions which, in gifted and advanced practitioners, can lead to altered states of consciousness. However, it is all too easy to forget that these are mere ideas, which we may have made into fascinating and consoling mind pictures. They then become, in effect, evasions, in that they make it more difficult to sustain a *don't know* mind, empty and open to receive whatever gifts of insight may be offered. The ancient Ch'an scripture *On Trust in the Heart* warns us that, of death and all the grave and constant concerns of life, "the more you think about it, the more you talk about it, the further from it you go. Put an end to wordiness and intellection and there is nothing you will not understand. For what can words tell of that which has no yesterday, tomorrow or today?" Similarly, many centuries later, the great Zen master Dogen, who emphasised death as the central concern and practice, urged us not to analyse it or speak about it. "Just set aside your body and mind, forget about them, and throw them into the house of Buddha; then all is done by Buddha."

If we ask ourselves questions like "What is my death?" and "Where do I go after I die?" we may be able to come up with some interesting ideas. But in the shadow of death we shall need more than fascinating explanations to sustain us. Our salvation lies in sustaining holy ignorance, the open, receptive mind of bare awareness. This requires faith, courage and determination, because when we penetrate beyond i*deas* about dying we uncover what we really fear, and with good reason — our *feelings* about dying.

A Good Death?

In recent years there has been some shift away from the preoccupation with the spiritual and existential experience of death and dying towards bodily deterioration and its psychological and social implications. As we live longer more and more of us endure decades of low-level, chronic ill-health, often followed by prolonged terminal illness, from which we may be "rescued" time and time again by sophisticated medical interventions.

The classic "good death" is about the experience of acceptance and awareness – a kind of epiphany – in the final hours of life. However, Sherwin B. Nuland, in a pioneering critique, warned that "the comfort and peace, and especially the conscious serenity, of final lingering days on earth have been vastly overestimated by many commentators; we are not well served by being lulled into unjustified expectations." A survey by Karlis Osis of over 35,000 observations by doctors and nurses. concluded that only 10% of patients were even conscious in the hour before death. Of these only one in twenty (0.5% of the total) showed any signs of elation. We may surmise that many of them may in fact have rejoiced at no more than a merciful release from prolonged suffering.

Thus few of us are likely to enjoy the privilege of the "good death". It is true that within certain limits we *can* prepare for how we shall die, and hence influence our experience of dying, but these limits are narrowly set by the nature of whatever kind of physical deterioration eventually afflicts us. We are most likely to die in a coma or under heavy sedation. Long before that the person who we recognisably are, to ourselves and to our friends and relations, may have become distorted almost beyond recognition.

It is true that advances and wider use of palliative treatment has led to more effective pain control. But this has in turn brought to the fore other afflictions which patients find frightening and depressing. There may be a crisis of identity: no longer able to recognise oneself, reinforced by the evident difficulty that the nearest and dearest may have in treating you as the person they once knew and loved. Also there is the frightening lack of bodily control and ability to sustain dignity when reduced to helplessness by vomiting, incontinence, and the like.

There is now a growing awareness of the very diverse ways in which people evolve through terminal illness and approach their deaths. Researchers have claimed that as the hospice movement has grown, what were the creative and flexible perspectives of the founders have tended to become institutionalised stereotypes, in both training and care. The good death, they claim, has become a benchmark, even an "ideology", against which patients can be measured, as also the stages through which they are supposed to pass in getting to it. Those, for example, who remain in denial may be considered the awkward and unsatisfactory ones, who subtly threaten the equanimity of the staff by not doing what they are supposed to do and not dying by the book. This can amount to a discriminatory lack of respect for some patients' autonomy, and has provoked calls for greater concern for that autonomy.

The above critique suggests that there may be a something of a contemporary Western Buddhist *ideology* of death, an idealisation which has tended to obscure the diverse realities of dying. The following testimony from Frank Ostaseski, administrator of the 1992 San Francisco Zen Hospice Project, is worth bearing in mind:

> However many dying people I have known, this person is dying for the first time and I don't know what they need: everyone has different needs. You must hold your previous experience of dying patients very lightly, so if they prove incorrect for this person you can shift very quickly.

In the light of the above I believe it is now time for a shift away from the final hours of the "good death" to an emphasis on the good life. How we have lived is more important than how we die, over which we may very well have little or no control. More particularly, whatever our dying lot turns out to be, we can as from now prepare ourselves by the practice of bare awareness described earlier. Through this we can make the experience of our terminal afflictions more manageable and endurable, and can longer sustain our personal integrity. In dropping all illusion and evasion this can indeed be a time of insight and transformation, and in this sense a true culmination of the life we have lived.

Thus, in her excellent book *Making Friends with Death*, Judith Lief advises:

> When death occurs, our old strategies no longer apply, so we are disorientated and frightened. How can we work with this? How can we better prepare ourselves to deal with death? The best preparation is working with our state of mind *now* rather than thinking about exotic things we might do later when we are looking death in the eyes. It is better to learn to relate to death now, when we still have the strength and ability... People have different paths and different teachers and different traditions — but whatever our tradition is, it is not going to help us very much if we don't actually apply it. The point is: do it now; don't wait.

Lief advises working with the many smaller "deaths" we encounter day by day, year by year, ranging from losing a favourite pen to losing someone we love, from missing a train to receiving a fateful diagnosis — all the many shocks and losses of life. Such an awareness practice prepares for facing the greatest of the self's losses — of itself, of its life.

There are No Old People in this Room!

"There is no time. What is memory?" This intriguing and beautiful question is inscribed on a temple arch in Hong Kong. It compassionately challenges our conventional view of time which moves forward through youth, ageing and death. It invites us to experience time in a way that is unfamiliar but which is no less true.

From this viewpoint our past can only exist embodied in some way in the present — such as a memory recalled to mind, or an entry in a diary, a picture in a family photo album. Similarly the future can only exist as it is imagined in the present. In this sense there is only the present. And so we are neither young nor old and we are not growing older either; we are just who we are now. In this sense, in a room of old age pensioners, there are no old people.

This mode of experiencing who we are can be very liberating if it is taken deeply to heart. This *suchness* of our situation has been distilled in music, poetry, and art.

However, the present resembles Euclid's definition of a line: it has no thickness. (And, in terms of conventional, relative truth it is an endlessly moving line.). So not only do we have no past or future, we have no present either!

Similarly, we are accustomed to experiencing our embodiment in certain conventional ways — like as a reflection in a mirror. But a biologist, a chemist or a physicist would have very different representations of a human body. Not only does our self have no time; there is no substantiality about it either. So, what is this mystery?

And yet it is no less true that we set our alarm clock to wake us in the morning, and that we then have to get this body out of bed. So, from another aspect, there *is* time, there *is* substance. And yet they are "empty" of time and substance. This paradox is sometimes called in Buddhism the doctrine of the two truths. It cannot be understood by any amount of thinking about it. We can only experience with our "don't know" mind, what it is to live timelessly in time, and to be old and yet neither-old-nor-young. We can live beyond life-and-death, and yet still age and die. As the *Heart Sutra* says: "...No withering nor death, nor end of them..."

In such life-and-death we truly are at home — or whatever you wish to call it: the Tao, the Universe, the Buddha Mind. Life and death have been likened to a great waterfall. For a brief moment the water of the river is flung out in isolated droplets, drawn down and down by the pull of gravity. Finally with a crash they come together to form the great river again.

Is it not strangely arrogant and irrational for us "to rage against the fading of the light", against our ageing and death, when everything else blooms, fades and dies? Why do we distress ourselves with this futile lawsuit against how it is, when it is within our power to drop this illusion that we are somehow not part of a perpetually changing reality? Here, in the ageing of this embodied self and the prospect of death, when evasion has become so difficult, we are confronted with the great opportunity finally to fulfil our human potential.

4 — Celebration

Finally, let us not neglect the celebration of old age, which gets less prominence in our culture than either the bad news or the ever-youthful evasions of it. What we celebrate is the accumulated wisdom of just having lived so long. As opposed to the negativity of ageism this is our contribution to a fast moving culture which is becoming increasingly disorientated.

For my part I am deeply grateful to have made it through seventy-three years. There's doubtless more to come yet, but I do feel a sense of completion in looking back down the travelled road, and all that has been learnt, achieved and contributed.

There are, of course, also the follies, regrets and wrong turnings. But, by old age, if we have been guilty we have now been guilty for long enough, and it is time to close any unfinished business both with people whom we feel we have wronged and those we believe have wronged us. Now or never is the time to make peace with our past. One by one we need to invite these people in (alive or dead), and visualize ourselves standing in their shoes, listening to what they need to say. We can then offer our final apologies or forgiveness.

We should not dismiss or condone the ingrained follies which may have disfigured our lives. But after we have made whatever atonement is called for we should let them go. Otherwise they can continue to shackle us with a guilt which can disable the creative opportunities of our old age. And if we continue to blame others we may perversely prefer to go on living with such an obsession rather than facing the scary freedom of taking full responsibility for ourselves. I believe it is healing to *honour* at least some of our follies, even as we regret them, as having their own logic in the unfolding of our lives.

There is much to celebrate about the inner resources we now have and which we probably lacked in earlier years. There is the self-reliance which comes from having weathered so many of the storms of life. There is also a deeper appreciation of the complexity of life's situations, and of their problematic character. This makes for greater tolerance, wiser solutions, and amused detachment. And for many, life is lived more of a piece, in contrast to the separate and sometimes conflicting roles which we may have had to sustain when younger.

There is an old French proverb, *vient la mort on danse*, as death approaches we can dance. By now we have probably done most of the things we are *supposed* to do and *ought* to do. At last we are *free*, variously, to idle, to contemplate, to explore, to take risks, to take off — all in a relaxed and creative way. How very sad if we continue to drive ourselves with all our old habitual imperatives, on which we may have covertly become so dependent that we may have difficulty giving them up.

What a pity to have had the good fortune to have lived to be so old and yet to remain trapped in who we were, without being able to step out into the new life that awaits us!

> A single moon
>
> Bright and clear
>
> In an unclouded sky:
>
> Yet still we stumble
>
> In the world's darkness
>
> — Zen Master Ikkyu

References and Readings

The Buddha's parable of the two arrows will be found in the *Samyutta-nikaya*, xxxvi.6 (the *Sallatha Sutta*), from which this is a free translation.

John Welwood "'Befriending Emotion", in John Welwood, ed., *Awakening the Heart: Eastern and Western Approaches to Psychotherapy and the Healing Relationship*(Boulder:Shambhala, 1983, pp84-90).

Venerable Nyanaponika Mahathera *The Power of Mindfulness*(Kandy: Buddhist Publication Society, 1976, (Wheel Publication 121/122), p16).

Chögyam Trungpa *The Myth of Freedom* (Boulder: Shambhala, 1976, p70).

Hubert Benoit *The Supreme Doctrine* (New York: Viking, 1959, p239).

Elisabeth Kübler-Ross *On Death and Dying* (New York:Macmillan, 1969).

Stephen Levine *Who Dies? An Investigation of Conscious Living and Conscious Dying* (Bath: Gateway Books, 1988 Ch. 10 "Working with Pain").

Larry Rosenberg *Living in the Light of Death: the Art of Being Truly Alive* (Boston: Shambhala, 2000).

Sogyal Rinpoche *The Tibetan Book of Living and Dying* (San Francisco: Harper San Francisco, 1992).

XinXinMing "On Trust in the Heart". Probably the most widely translated of Ch'an (Zen) scriptures, this poem is attributed to Seng ts'an (c.600CE). The translation here is mainly from Arthur Waley, in Edward Conze and others, *edsBuddhist Texts throughout the Ages* (Oxford: Cassirer, 1954).

Eihei Dogen *Shobogenzo: Zen Essays by Dogen* translated and edited by Thomas Cleary (Honolulu: University of Hawaii Press, 1986. "Birth and death" (*Shoji*), pp121-123).

Sherwin B. Nuland *How we Die* (London: Chatto & Windus, 1994).

Karlis Osis *At the Hour of Death* (New York: Avon Books, 1979).

For research and discussion critical of "the ideology of the good death" and its effect upon the autonomy of the dying, see Tony Walter *The Revival of Death* (London: Routledge, 1994) (from which the Frank Ostaseski quotation has been taken, p108); Julia Lawton *Patients' Experience of Palliative Care* (London: Routledge, 2000); and Bethne Hart & others "Whose dying? A sociological critique of the 'good death'" (*Mortality*, 3(1) 1998, pp65-77).

Judith Lief *Making Friends with Death* (Boston: Shambhala, 2001).

The concluding poem by the 15th century Zen Master Ikkyu is taken from *Wild Ways: Zen Poems of Ikkyu*, edited and translated by John Stevens (Boston: Shambhala, 1995, p107).

Literary Zen: Haiku and Haibun

The *dō* or way of haiku is among the traditional Japanese arts the practice of which enhances and supplements Zen Buddhist practice, along with calligraphy, martial arts, flower arrangement and the like. Haiku in the classic Japanese tradition are like tiny coiled springs which offer a sudden insight and release from the root anxiety and sense of lack from which human beings typically suffer. In their concrete just-how-it-is-ness and selflessness they can offer a heartfelt sense of acceptance and relief from the needy self in hardy times. They offer the reader an open-ended metaphor recalling the playful spaciousness of Zen.

The empty chair

the open book

this still life

In their understated allusion, their paradox, irony, black comedy, and ambiguity they nurture a Zen sensibility, whether in the writing or the reading.

Zen

in the raked gravel

a paw mark

For more, see my essays "Liberative Haiku" and "Zen and the Art of Haiku" in my website, www.kenjoneszen.com. The above two haiku are taken from my collection *The Parsley Bed*.

The most challenging of Zen haiku are undoubtedly those of Nagata Koi, which I have presented in the following essay.

Nagata Koi — "A *Haijin* from Hell"

Of Zen haiku poets, Nagata Koi (1900-1997), in his Mahayana Buddhism, is particularly demanding. Here we find ourselves on the wilder shores of existentially liberative haiku. "We can call haiku religious in the sense that it is always a means of seeking for a way to live, and to discover and express truth, goodness and beauty."

I have relied here on a bilingual selection of a hundred of Nagata's haiku with the warning title of *A Dream like this World*, translated by Naruto Nana and Margaret Mitsutani. The book also contains examples of Nagata's unique styles of calligraphy and ink painting — widely admired and much exhibited. Scattered throughout are brief statements about the nature of haiku. Like — "The true writer is a writer from hell." Nagata was undoubtedly a major figure on the Japanese cultural scene, though more admired by post-modern poets than by many in the conservative haiku community

There are two barriers to the full appreciation of Nagata's haiku. Their translation is made the more difficult by his use of made-up words and compounds, much like Eihei Dogen, the great thirteenth-century Zen philosopher-monk whom he so much admired. Some haiku seem quite banal, raising a doubt that we may be losing something in translation:-

a black icicle

my slip up

but what a sight!

There are others which strike the English reader as little more than truisms:

a cat in heat dedicates himself to

love

The linguistic fog mingles with the philosophic fog of *sunyatta* or "emptiness" — the key doctrine of Mahayana Buddhism, at the heart of so many of Nagata's haiku. For our purpose, that refers to the "suchness", the "just-how-it-isness" when we experience something without reference to anything else. For example, at times we may experience our self as simply who we are without reference to being "old now", or "still young". At that moment we step out of fleeting time and into timeless time (though both are equally "real") Here are two instances from Nagata:

I cut a lily	a morning glory
time stops	one hundred visits
like a flying arrow	and my mother will die

Typically the anxious self, with its ingrained sense of "lack", is always wanting, in matters great and small, for it to be "this" (which will sustain its sense of a solid identity) and not "that" (which will threaten it). The great Buddhist teacher, Krishnamurti, on the stage before a large audience, once raised his hand to show the gap between thumb and forefinger. He then delivered his lecture: "Ladies and gentlemen! All the miseries of the world are created by that gap — between 'this' and 'that'! "Contrariwise, when we are able to dwell in suchness, beyond this dualism,we live at ease with both self and others. This is what Nagata is attempting to communicate in a significant number of his haiku.

Let us consider first this simple example of Nagata's nondual vision and let it come alive in our imagination.

a winter crow

steps forward

the scene steps with him

Instead of seeing the crow as separate from the surrounding landscape we are invited here to experience both as a single happening.

A further step is where we playfully dissolve the dualism of the "real" versus the "unreal", as in surrealism. Nowadays, surreal haiku are by no means rare. Here is one from Nagata:

furrows

left alone to play

in the moonlight

But surely furrows don't play? Maybe they do, if left alone by folks for whom a dull day at the office remains "real" as compared with the "unreality" of a vivid and transformative dream that they had the previous night. Likewise we may encounter a painting which quite transcends our customary "real" experience of that very same subject. And what if drifting cloud in moonlight, the play of light and shade, were to set those furrows dancing?

"How could you find anything more concrete than ideas?" exclaims Nagata. He continues:

> I believe that poetry is what changes existence into illusion. Or you might say it changes reality into illusion. In my old age I find myself using all reality — especially the reality surrounding human beings; even this aging body I see before my eyes — as the dream of reality, or the reality of the dream, and this gives me a peculiar sense of joy. In the highest sense, life is illusion.

And so...

how lonely!

cultivating stone leeks

in this world of dreams

This is in fact a translation by James Kirkup and Makoto Tamati which catches the spirit of the poet particularly well. As with a Zen koan, best chewed ruminatively, or maybe swallowed in one gulp. Dissect it and it becomes a dead thing. But does not life sometimes feel a lonely and bleak affair of unrewarding effort, where "reality" itself becomes nightmarish? And may not this feeling give expression to life's just-how-it-isness in a single breath? And may not this shared experience, so poignantly expressed, lift the burden a little?

the guts age first

the skylark

soars

Nagata is urging a single experience here, not two — a good and a bad. So it is was with our own Cockney mystic, William Blake: "Joy and woe are woven fine, a clothing for the soul divine."

Here is a haiku on which Nagata himself offers a commentary:

an old cat straining, shits —

in such a pose

my mother dies in winter

One day in a wasteland I had plowed myself I saw an old cat crouched in a frozen furrow taking a shit. God's transparent wing covered the scene like a veil. But I was able to see everything through it. For a long time I watched the hunched up body of that aged cat, seeing in it the primal form of the existence to which it must naturally return. The actual length of time is irrelevant to metaphysical intuition, but you might say that with the eyes of eternity I was witnessing an eternal truth. It had nothing to do with either beauty or virtue. It was truth itself; poetry itself.

In several of the haiku the suchness of their subjects is expressed very explicitly. Suppose you were suddenly to come upon an old bottle lying neglected on the ground and evidently still containing some liquid. For a moment the "this or that" mind may not register whether the liquid is "cloudy" or "transparent", or some halfway state either. There is a momentary release from the bondage of words, allowing things to stand forth in their own right:

old square bottle

all

transparent and cloudy

Nagata's output is diverse, and there are many poems which make a ready impact without resort to Buddhist decoding.

a weary man

lost in thought

an aged butterfly

between his thighs

Or, arguably on the same theme of impotent old age:

the autumn wind —

in my belly

the face of a maiden

The overall impression of this collection is of a playfulness typical of Zen, where nothing is quite what it seems, but which can help us to ride more loosely in life's saddle. The book is full of "laughing catfish" which pop up all over the place:-

my joints laugh with the catfish

wriggling in my hands

A Dream Like This World: One Hundred Haiku by Nagata Koi, translated by Nana Naruto and Margaret Mitsutani. Nana Naruto, 4-3-6, Toyosumi, Kashiwa, Chiba, 277-0071 (Japan: 2000). With grateful acknowledgement.

Haibun and Zen

My own particular interest has been in haibun. This is an ancient Japanese genre now flourishing in the West, and comprising haiku-like prose enhanced by intermittent haiku. I have written some two hundred in all, most published in various journals and also in a series of books: *Arrow of Stones* (British Haiku Society,2002); *Stallion's Crag* (Iron Press, 2003); *The Parsley Bed* (Pilgrim Press, 2006); *Stone Leeks* (Pilgrim Press,2009) and *Bog Cotton*. (Alba Publishing, 2012). They have attracted a variety of awards. Virtually all are imbued, more or less, with a Zen spirit and characteristics which have grown more evident over the years.

Those I have selected below have two themes. The first nine have retreats as their subject. The remainder trace out to date my ageing through a long drawn-out terminal cancer.

Solitary Retreats

The Grey Stone (2002)
(Stallion's Crag)

Father Time on the weathervane

WSW

scything over green fields

Y Maen Llwyd — The Grey Standing Stone. Gives its name to a small farmhouse folded into the Radnorshire hills. Around a muddy yard are sheep pens and a barn, now a meditation hall surmounted by a weathervane. All silent and empty for my seven day solitary in the lean-to. *KLONDYKE* is embossed in cast iron on the stove.

Lightness of spruce

little dried blocks

iron belly

There is room enough for shrine, cushion, camp bed, desk, and easy chair. The other occupant is a winter fly, who sleeps upside down above the stove. Each morning, two hours before dawn, she and I and the pot belly all come to life together

The wind whistles

the stove grumbles back

between them

I sit

Out for a pee under a starlit sky. One face of the cheesy moon is already lit up by the sun rising, I suppose, somewhere over England. Owls return to their roosts in the dingle. Back on my cushion, vast space.

Later, I sit at the little desk...

Morning star

hiss of the pressure lamp

the sutras black on white

Turning off the lamp, staring out of the window.

Restless buzzing —

dawn filters slowly

through ragged clouds

The bliss of morning coffee is not mentioned in the sutras. Nor marmalade on toast. I brush my teeth, and get into Dogen's *Life and Death*.

Along the track another of my kind greets me. "Nice day, it is!" The care-worn face of a farmer, heaving a dead ewe into the trailer. Later, in fading light, I wander up onto the hill. Shoulders hunched, searching as usual for something too shy to show itself. Hands tighten on the rust of an iron gate.

Warmed by the setting sun

my skinny shadow

stretching across a field

Down in the valley the searchlight of an occasional car, swinging round a bend. And then ... against the evening sky, there it is.

Again that thorn tree

rooted to the spot

standing and staring

Again the old fool is reminded. Doffs his cap, and bows to the tree. For only when the self retires do the ten thousand things advance and enlighten.

The Maen Llwyd is an electricity free zone, apart from my torch. It picks out this and that as a flood of light can never do. Once, a fly.

Down on paper —

drawn to the torchlight heart

transparent speckled wings

And later a hatchet…

Old axe

the sway

in its haft

Here are two centuries of heat and light. There is the generous soft light of the Victorian lamp, the ultimate in paraffin technology and elegance. And the battered *VALOR* heater, recalling the draughty bed sits of my youth. The oldest exhibit stands with a box of Co-op matches beside my bed.

Made for thick fingers

pewter candleholder

its brass snuffer

Down in the valley lies Pant-y-Dwr — the Watery Hollow of some ninety souls, with the lowest temperatures in Wales, and its most central pub, the Mid Wales Inn. A ghostly moon, veiled in mist, floats above the nine sodium lights.

I throw more logs into the stove, pump up the flaring Tilley lamp, and heat a can of baked beans.

Closing curtains

opening curtains

this long life

of nights and days

Later, I light a single candle before the pale green figure of Kwan Yin, goddess of compassion, austere and erect. A slender stick of pine incense perfumes the air. Three times the sounding bowl ripples the silence, and the first watch of the night begins. An hour passes, and I stretch my legs across the passage in the cold shadows of the meditation hall. On the other side of the yard the weather-beaten planks of the old barn are silver bright.

Slow pacing meditation

reassuringly

a floor board creaks

Returning, I wrap my black robe about me and ease my body into the last sit of the day. The short chant has a depth and richness that takes me unaware. Kuan Yin stares back, with that elusive smile of hers.

In the murmuring stove

soft cry of owls

incense

burnt out

Trekking Poles (2004)
(*The Parsley Bed*)

A dream, a lightning flash, or cloud

So should we view this world

— The Buddha

Mountain tent

cold and sleepless

I unpick the years of my life

To a tattoo of hailstones I unzip this, my twenty-seven thousandth mortal day. In the dawn light a damp, gleaming still life of odds and ends lies heaped in the bell end of the tent. A solitary stonechat sings a little song. Yet all this began in sunshine...

Climbing the mountain for the umpteenth time

striding shadows

of my trekking poles

But then holed up by unseasonable weather. At freezing point the little stove struggles to boil water for my coffee. I wrap my hand round the cold gas cylinder, and it hisses louder.

Crawling arthritically out of the tent, I remember to turn sharp left above the hundred foot drop that is just outside. I have abandoned the neighbouring damp cave of saints, poets and warriors. It serves now only as an oratory, a flickering bright refuge in a howling wilderness, where I chant the morning and evening office. The cast iron Buddha has his hand raised in benediction, until he too will rust away. Sometimes there is a little company to be had here…

In candlelight

a scuttling beetle

her shiny back

At dawn and dusk I climb up above the cave onto the flat slate top of Stallion's Crag. From here Owain Glyndwr evaded his English pursuers and leapt from history into myth.

A hero's war horse

hoof prints set in stone

my walking meditation

Twenty-one brisk circumambulations around the edge. Down through craggy pinnacles, in mist and thin rain, stretches the great trackless valley where no one comes.

Today I must leave, struggling against the wind across the ridge and down the spur to the road-head an hour and a half away. Back through the magic door. On which side lies the dream?

Everything moves on —

the drifting shadows

of clouds

The Question (2005)
(*The Parsley Bed*)

Skyline far off

the fretted gate

always there

As in some obsessive love affair, I am drawn back again and again. This lonely strip of water, now black, now silver, now prussian blue. Here I sit and pace the shoreline, night and day.

Sixteen hundred feet up. Lost on a moor of heather covered knolls, of textured browns and greens and yellows, sour bogs and black peat hags. My little world apart — this solitude of ruffled water, circumnavigated in all of half an hour. The way round the lake is barred at one end by a livid green tongue thrust out through the tawny moorland. Across it, humping and squelching, I lay a trail of stepping stones

My weight on a stone

the whole bog

shudders and quakes

I have grown fond of these bogs. They have attitude.

Each little tussock

celebrating tussockness

its own way

The stony shoreline is bright with lichens. At one end rises a miniature cliff, sheltering a pine — the only tree for miles. The lake is fed by a stream, falling into an elegant bathing pool before finally tumbling into the lake. Nearby is a rough stone shelter, piled up a hundred years ago or more by some other lover of the lake. It has been cunningly curved against the sneaking winds.

> In the stone shell of a snail
>
> curled up cosy
>
> on my bilberry bed

Tŷ Malwoden — the Snail House. Out on the point I have raised a cairn. Its white quartz cap catches the first and the last sun of each day — however rarely offered. From beneath an angler's umbrella I flick the question back and forth across my mind, with never a bite. Deftly shied, my slates skip and skim, but never reach the other shore.

This afternoon I take my wanting mind and needy heart for a stroll around our world. A pale shadow turns up to complete the party. A Greek chorus of wild-fowl chortle and chuckle in the reeds. And the wind blows as usual.

> Clattering over
>
> shards of slate
>
> to make my presence felt

However, by the time we have returned to where we began all of us feel the better for it. The heart has eased, the mind stopped fidgeting, the shadow a richer black. Also, there is the discovery, in different places, of three magic boulders. Once settled on them, all agitation dies away, and there is only the sweet song of the wind and the waves. Each I mark with a quartz stone.

And by night time the wind has fallen. The question is forgotten.

> A crescent moon
>
> comes floating
>
> on a raft of stars

The morning after…

On a boulder, where the stream flows into the lake. Between the babble of the brook and the lapping of the waves —

A skeleton

breathing air

and pumping blood

Here Now (2013)
(after *Bog Cotton*)

On this black robe

the dust of incense

silent thunder

The darkness before dawn. Fumbling for the matchbox, the candle holder. Bare feet on a stone floor. Shivering in my thick Welsh flannel shirt. Fired up, the pot bellied stove roars up the flue pipe. In an hour the black kettle will sing. From its cupboard I drag the white wash bowl, splashing a jug of stream water on the emblazoned Prince of Wales' feathers.

Another candle and Gwan Yin, the goddess of compassion, comes to life amid a waft of sandalwood incense. The dawn vows growl deep in the belly.

Three strikes

on the brass bowl

echoing silence

On the black cushion the body sits tall, the shoulders fall, the breathing slows. Only the murmur of the stream, the muttering of the stove. Time and place dissolve.

In harsh dawn light a new day. The snow has come. Porridge and black coffee, they never taste so good as this.

"'What is Zen?' The Master replies: 'Chopping wood and drawing water'". So out to my wood stack and the clear spring nearby.

In the snow

fox and hare

their mingled tracks

Noon and the bliss of lentil soup into which I've chopped Carmarthen "sausages".

And so it is, day following day, as the snow begins to thaw. Taking mind for walks in the forest, and stretching on the yoga mat to keep it at home in the body. Every night —

My empty slippers

each one

freed to be itself

The familiar surroundings in the cabin are vividly made new. Miraculously the protests and irritations of an eighty-three year old body go unnoticed. The fears of an old man nearing his end melt away into simply how it is.

This dull damp day

light reflected in a rain drop

dangling from a briar

Group Retreats

Putting Legs on a Snake (2004)
(The Parsley Bed)

Hazy moon

the rusty weathervane

clanks and groans

A brief, broken sleep, spilling vivid dreams, and leaving a metallic taste beneath the tongue. The hour before dawn, lit by one large candle. One by one the black robed figures file in. They bow to a hall of shadows. They bow to their meditation cushions. They bow to one another. Their bows knit darkness and light. *Clack! Clack!* — wooden clappers hasten the stragglers. On the walls we face our tall unsteady shadows.

Silence settles, and then a rustle at the door. The Master pads in; does his rounds. A board creaks as his heavy shadow passes by. Palms joined, our chant growls deep in the belly:

All evil karma ever committed by me

On account of my beginningless greed, anger and ignorance

Born of my body, mouth and thought

Now I atone for it all

The last line dies away mournfully. Minds turn inwards: the contemplation of Mind. Legs locked, I sit rooted on my cushion. At first, old films in the skull cinema — the usual serials, docu-soaps, and trailers. Boring. The reel slows, the pictures fade...

Faint streaks of dawn across the sky. Pale light begins to fill the hall. Far away some small bird repeats its creaky one-note call.

Window pane

a bluebottle crawls unsteadily

towards the morning star

A choreographed breakfast. Three nested oryoki bowls, chop sticks, a spoon, a scraper, various cloths are manipulated to the sound of chants, bells and clappers, accompanied by tea and porridge. At first, tiresomely complicated; once mastered, elegant simplicity. Strong green tea, steaming shadows on the polished floor.

The servers alone can indulge in a little exhibitionism. Brenda, from Liverpool, comes flouncing in, her sash tied up behind in a great bow. Sure footed beneath the hem of her robe, she bears aloft a porringer, the head of John the Baptist. For me, her fellow Scowse, a coquettish bow, a sly wink.

Prancing *dakini*

a string of grinning skulls

preserves her modesty

Samu – work period. Round the back, in thin rain, I scrape away at a wall that has already been scraped. Mindfully. Ignoring the rule of silence my fellow scraper introduces herself as the editor of an Australian fashion magazine. Inhaling deeply, we share a limp roll up and chat about Enlightenment.

The Zen day gets seriously under way. The liturgy: bare feet on black mats.

That bald old monk

the way he offers incense

all there is to know

I know that man. Young German communist, tortured by the Gestapo. For us Buddhist Bolsheviks, old soldiers of past lives, the road is long, the gratitude is deep.

Soapstone Buddha

an archaic smile

last of the incense

Afterwards the Master delivers his morning *teisho*. My German friend and I sit flanking him like impassive China dogs. "To light your lamp in broad daylight and go rummaging around for what stands right before you is black comedy indeed!" Some of us knit our brows; others try to look Enlightened. Comedians with sore legs, sitting eight hours a day, locked in one kind of lotus or another. Only the Liverpool woman voices disagreement. She's fond of him.

A long sit.

In the corridor

worn shoes lined up

each pair itself

The *jikijitsu* prowls down the seated ranks. First the raised shadow of his "wake up stick" , then his pink feet. From time to time he stops to straighten backs, adjust hands. "Don't sniff!", he roars, "Just dribble!" **"WAKE UP!"** *Thwack! Thwack!* Then we hear the stick being placed back in front of the Buddha and a heavy body easing itself onto its cushion. We enjoy a bit the peace. A fly alights; tiptoes round my skull; is gone.

At the end of the lane

that goes nowhere

dappled sunlight

"Dokusan! Interviews! Move!" I am trampled in the youthful rush. Out in the corridor the interview line strains and sweats out the meaning of life. Inside the Master's room, incense and aftershave. Nothing to lose, I grow frisky and congratulate him on this seven day production of the Theatre of the Absurd. Each day waiting for Godot. He comes clean. "An idiot captain of a ship of fools".

Wandering about; kicking stones; seeking Enlightenment still.

Torchlight —

in the White Rabbit's burrow

a stately mushroom

Notes:

Hazy moon: symbolizes enlightenment.

Morning star: signalled the Buddha's great awakening.

Scouse: from Liverpool.

Dakini: a Tantric goddess.

One kind of lotus or another: meditation posture; most can manage "a quarter lotus".

Jikijitsu: disciplinarian in the Rinzai Zen tradition.

Love and Silence (2009)
(*Bog Cotton*)

One by one the retreatants arrive. Sip tea. Hang about. Guarded. Expectant. I gather them in a circle of black cushions. They eye one another. And they eye me, and my premature smile. The first talk opens with a silence, not too long not too short. To every phrase its own space. Hopefully I scan the faces for signs of making sense. It takes time to draw them in, one by one, for our journey to begin.

Worn clipboard

the spring still grips

my scribbled thoughts

Before dawn, the Crack! Crack! of the wake-up clappers. Muffled figures shuffle into the yard, with its hissing lamps and pools of rainwater. Following my creaky gestures, our physical jerks begin. And then some watchwords for the day.

Wind-blown —

an empty can

rattles over cobbles

Back inside I glance along the lines of meditators. An awesome stillness hangs in the air. To each skull cinema its own films: old news reels, future trailers, or maybe the big picture itself. Or even a blank screen. Or perhaps the projectionist has already gone home? Through lidded eyes, downward gaze at forty-five degrees. Ah! I see him steal a restless glance. And she gets the message.

Retreat romance

ripened

by the rule of silence

Interviews, one by one. Together we watch the sky turn pale above the great field. Through a fretted line of trees a tiny light. She fingers the stitching of her leather chair. And starts to tell me…

By the second evening the retreat has taken on a life of its own, and carries us along with it. Inside, as well as outside, the weather is what it needs to be.

Into our shared silence

a howling wind

a beating rain

I have them gather in groups of four around a "speaking stone." To share with one another each their unwinnable lawsuit against reality. And perhaps to empty their hearts.

Cupping the hand-warmed stone

feeling its jagged edges

he lets it speak

Five days of gathered silence. Enough to thaw the love between strangers.

The group photo includes the Goddess of Compassion in black teak. From her shrine she is looking over someone's shoulder, a hand raised in blessing.

Hard Up (2014)
(after *Bog Cotton*)

Dang! Dang! Dang!

dreams and dreamlessness

broken alike

She bustles along the dimly-lit corridor, clanging her cow bell. The indoor retreatants clamber out of their iron bunks. The campers emerge out of the mist. A few grateful sips of black coffee — or peppermint tea.

In the hall the candles cast giant shadows on the walls. Amid wafts of sandalwood incense the stone Buddha raises one hand in blessing; the other touches the earth.. Each retreatant is already settled on his or her black cushion, and the awesome stillness of a meditation hall stops me at the door.

I settle myself between a Yorkshire drystone waller and a trade union organiser from Hackney. For this is a Zen "Freely Given" retreat for those who are hard-up, to crack that invisible Buddhist middle-class ceiling.

The ferocity of the storm batters the stone building, sending in draughts which threaten to dowse the candle which lights our shrine. Alert and calm, not one of the retreatants flinches. I recall the griefs and courage of their personal predicaments, unfolded yesterday in the interview room.

Thunder and lightning at dawn

the light within the dark

of the Great Way

Interviews on Group Retreats
(Names and other details disguised to conceal identities)

Two High Backed Chairs (2007)
(Stone Leeks)

By firelight

The Lives of the Saints

bound in leather

In our black robes we have filed back from Evensong across the cathedral close. "You should come more often", says the canon, who welcomes our Zen retreat in the Deanery. I leave the candle-lit meditation hall to prepare for interviews here in the library. Pale evening light filters through the tall Georgian windows, and the sandalwood incense wafts a different odour of sanctity. On a side table the Goddess of Compassion raises her hand in blessing above a box of Kleenex tissues.

Wind scoured beach

to every tiny pebble

its tail of sand

Jack

Young and earnest, all in black, he pads in, sporting a martial arts t-shirt. His designer stubble is well maintained and he takes us both very seriously. I try him with a few playful sallies, but he hangs on to his shop lifted goods. A nice lad in a Zen mask, taken in for further questioning.

In its little cage

a clockwork bird

wound up

Jane

Halting steps, a timid knock, a growl of welcome. Thin and anxious, her clothes dowdy, her hair lank. Life frightens her. But she is brave enough to come here. She and I, we take a kindly interest in her fear. She loves William Blake. "Joy and woe are woven fine". A wan smile lights up her face; she will be alright.

David

The stride of a well-established self. He has a degree in Buddhism and goes on about Zen. His Japanese pronunciation is impressive. I stare at his highly polished shoes and wait until he's finished. We shall have to turn out his pockets, to discover where he keeps his anger, his fear, and, hopefully, his love. I discover he is having difficulties at home, so we start there.

Climbing steeply

through storm clouds

fly on the window

Amy

Red salopettes and long blond hair. The way she moves, she knows a thing or two. She also knows that I know she's just called in to share the cosmic joke, or something of that sort. Playfully, I try to test her sense of humour to destruction, but we end up laughing again.

My false teeth mug

filled to overflowing

with her yellow flowers

Martha

Sensibly dressed and impaled on virtue. She has so much to do. Peace and justice. Children and aged parents. A husband, too. And enlightenment on top of all that. I invited her to reflect on the fact that Nothing matters; everything matters — which is also giving her a hard time. However, she has taken up singing. There is a singing woman deep inside. But still, as yet...

Round and round

the squirrel woman

in the wheel she's made

Martha's the last one for tonight. In the silence the cathedral clock gathers its strength and strikes ten times, each stroke a little less than perfect. Tears spring in my eyes..

Where sweet water

meets the rising tide

a tang of salt

A Room with a View (2013)
(after *Bog Cotton*)

A fading sickle moon

the dawn sun

creeping through the trees

My eyes fill with tears at the wonder of it. With a sigh I turn to the glow and waft of my incense, sip the last of the coffee, and settle myself down.. A hesitant knock; a growling "Come in."

"Relationships" — an unconventional Zen Buddhist retreat. Mainly women — aged from twenty-seven to seventy-two. The youngest are for me the challenge, occupying a time scarcely imaginable from the rear view of my eighty-three years.

First in the interview line this morning is Anthea, so needy and self-absorbed as to be almost beyond my reach. At thirty, she tells me, her life is in ruins. A pitiful story of failed relationships. Next to her, beside the Kleenex, sits the impassive Goddess of Compassion. Listening to Anthea, I feel like one of those mythic bodhisattvas drawn down into a hell of speed dating and tweeting as if it were a fairground — as in this case it appears to be for the inmates.

Quietly I repeat yesterday's meditation hall talk. This time I draw on our own Cockney mystic for help, with his breaking the "mind-forg'd manacles" and his "cleansing the doors of perception." Fogged up in her own grief and neediness, Anthea bows her head and listens dutifully.

Woodpecker

Great Spotted he,

echoing hollow through the woods

Somehow reaching us from back in AD600, the Third Zen Patriarch, Seng-ts'an, whispers a reminder from his great poem the *XinXinMing* "On Trust in the Heart" :-

The more you talk about it,

the more you think about it,

the further from it you go.

Put an end to wordiness and intellection

and there is nothing you will not understand

I chuckle to myself, and rise from my chair.

"Anthea, why not stand here and share the view from the window?" She does so. Ah, that little cry of surprised delight! And so for some minutes we stand side by side enjoying just how it is, sharing the trees and grasses, birds and flowers. Then she turns bright eyes to me. A kiss on the cheek. She hastens out, and the door closes with a soft click

I glance out of the window. The magic is visibly fading.

Strutting the gravel path

fanning his feathers

an ordinary peacock

Ageing towards Death

The Spirit Level (2001)
(*Arrow of Stones*)

Dedicated to fellow haijin John Crook, who died of cancer 16 April 2001

> *In this life*
> *we walk on the roof of hell*
> *and view the flowers*
>
> — Kobayashi Issa

"Next Wednesday — we'll phone the results to you between 4 and 5. Do you understand?"

After the biopsy, sweet coffee in a styrofoam cup. Driving home the familiar sunny hills are restless now with my unease. Five days to go. Five days to finish the summer house. Wednesday dawns fine.

> Coiling and drifting
>
> smoke
>
> from a new-lit fire
>
> sunbright blue

Just enough worn old bricks to build the steps. I watch myself loading the barrow with slow deliberation. Cement, buckets, the clatter of this and that. And the long bright spirit level. The mortar mix — not too stiff, not too sloppy. This trowelling of mortar is balm to the spirit. I lay the level across the finished slabs. The spirit bubble sits dead centre, between its two hair lines. How could it be otherwise? it says.

She has set out our lunch with care. Two polished glasses filled with sunlight; two white napkins rather unnerving. 3 o'clock. I potter at my desk. Outside, she listens to a neighbour who has been touched by Jesus. The dark green phone waits, silent in its cradle and unbelievable when it rings.

So sorry. It's cancer –

I go wring out the washing

hang it out to dry

Back to the summer house, trying not to disturb the new steps. Lock the door. Listen to the wind.

From west to east we flee together. To where the sun rises up from the sea instead of sinking into it. To where the world shrinks to a thin line between sky and fen. At Southwold, pints of Adnam's "Broadside" bitter. A jar of white honey from the Walberswick hives. Matins at Ely; evensong at Norwich.

Blackened niche

last year's nest

where a saint once stood

Home for more tests. The radiology unit has an air of carnival. What shall we play for you?

Bone scan

the length

of a Brandenburg Concerto

Judgement Day, at 11.30am. Yama, the bug-eyed Lord of Death, turns out to be a breezy fellow, an old school tie bright against his white coat. Obsequies seriously postponed. They can "help me live" at least until the end of the decade. I could even end up dying of something better. We celebrate at the Owl & Pussycat Tea-room. Sipping Earl Grey, I number the hairs of my head.

Returning home, we find visitors...

> Into the sadness
>
> a pair of mating ducks
>
> alighting on our pond

Yellow Petals (2005)
(*The Parsley Bed*)

> Simply trust:
>
> Do not the petals flutter down
>
> just like this?
>
> — Kobayashi Issa

PSA readings: 1.6... 2.4... 5.4... 5.8... 7.1... The mathematical ascent to death. Now slower, now faster, but always sure.

> Fear
>
> a rising curve
>
> through small blue squares

The ascending star of my would-be executioner — Basil, Basileus, imperial tumour of the prostate. A Good Death? "A spectacularly awful way to die", said one urologist — even when eased by the constipated nightmares of palliative morphine. Or perhaps a graceful exit by EasyJet to Zurich for a teatime appointment with Dr Death? Yet still a nightmare not yet metastised into reality.

The scabby walls of the cancer waiting room once displayed an exploded diagram of "The Genito-Urinary System", a tube map with the different parts brightly coloured, numbered and named — all ours. "It used to make me feel funny," says the bloke next to me, anxiously fingering his South Wales Echo. Then one day a big, black biro'd tumour appeared, with a smiley face, clutching the pink prostate. Now there's only art therapy on the walls. No Last Judgements by phlegmatic Flemings. Only Patience Strong stuff to match the brisk optimism of the doctors. "And how are we today, Mr... er...?"

Many of the patients here are ex-miners. Small, quiet, stoical men. No one makes a fuss. Resistance is futile. The late afternoon sun has sneaked round the corner of the hospice across the road. It floods in on us, a crowd of waiting men.

> The incense — ash
>
> the candle — melted grease
>
> yellow petals everywhere

Failed surgery or radiotherapy? Back on the conveyor belt as a "salvage" patient. Slow chemical castration then remains the only orthodox "treatment". Hardy souls opt out for a shorter life but a merrier one — if still up to it. The testosterone that feeds the cancer powers the passion.

> Together
>
> the wild laughter
>
> of abandonment

[Kobayashi Issa (1762-1826) was one of the great classic Japanese haiku masters.]

Going Nowhere (2006)
(*The Parsley Bed*)

How lonely!

Cultivating stone leeks

in this world of dreams

— Nagata Koi

For me two stone leeks on this freezing New Year's morning. First, the letter from Jack. It wasn't lumbago after all. The cancer has spread from the prostate and is now eating away his bones. And it has finished with our mutual friend Gerald, who passed away unpeacefully a few days ago. The second letter, from Australia, is his.

His final letter

that argumentative scrawl

to which there's no reply

A heavy overnight fall. Outside a world of whites and greys so still that I go out to touch it. In two elegant white curves my telephone line and my electricity sag high across the yard. The third musketeer, I unzip my flies and expertly flip the catheter tap.

Blood red urine

tracing in snow

the circle of infinity

I crunch across to the road gate. Through the shed window I catch a reassuring glimpse of the Apparatus which Jez and I assembled last week. All jubilee clips and small brass screws, built to last. He asked if he could have it after I'd finished with it. Code name GEM — Graceful Exit Machine, and deceptively simple. 1- Put on Bach CD; 2- Settle into familiar armchair; 3-

Don transparent plastic helmet; 4- Fix gaze on distant skyline of larches; 5- Twist the valve anti-clockwise. Arrival at Dontknowwhere guaranteed in 15 seconds. More heroic than being a morphine doped antelope eaten alive, hindquarters first, by that hungry lion. And yet... And yet...

Then my eye catches something beneath the window.

Frozen to death

bright eyes wide open

the Tragedy

of a Mouse

I set off up the track. Only a fox has been before me, smudging the deep snow with its brush. Summer motorists who get as far as the cottage ask where the track goes? Some get quite annoyed when I insist that it goes Nowhere. For a man in an armour-plated four-wheel drive there's always Somewhere. In fact it ends at the only completely empty kilometre square on the Ordnance Survey map. This morning the featureless plateau is just a blank white sheet, bearing only the faint prints of birds. I am disappointed. On a morning like this surely there should be a message pinned to the notice board? Then it struck me: I am the message! I chortle aloud; a passing raven chortles back.

Easier going home, and not only because it's downhill. A little black thing darts among the branches of the old damson tree. Whistling and piping, rich and sweet.

Weeping

for the blackbird

singing his love

Back home I wake up the stove and cut a slice of turkey pie. It sits there on its willow pattern plate. There's something reassuring about the sheer suchness of a slice of turkey pie.

Especially with home-made cranberry sauce, so I can even manage a couple of stone leeks with it.

It nerves me once again to update my life.

Correction fluid

across my dead friend's address

a white blanket

[The translation of Nagata Koi's haiku is by James Kirkup and Makoto Tamaki]

An Appointment with Yama (2010)
(*Bog Cotton*)

Vanishing in the smoke

of burning leaves

a weathered Buddha

At the Enno-ji temple in Kamakura the Lord of Death is in session with his ten officials at their desks. Hardwood carvings, life-sized. Not so much a judge and jury. More a data-processing unit of functionaries, assessing my life story and making the necessary karmic calculations for a favourable or unfavourable rebirth. For the terminally ill a waiting room is provided for creative writing, to pass the time.

EXIT sign

the intensity of waiting

at a revolving door

The past four years, on the first of each month, I have been presenting myself to one of the officials. He gives me that "Not you again!" look and, out of the side of his mouth, a decimal number. If the number — stable until now — has commenced to rise, the spell has broken and it's time to pack my bags. And so, on the last days of each month (like these) my sky begins to darken. Then — so far — it lightens again. And for about three weeks I can rejoin the throng who feel they are immortal.

Crazy fence

every barb

rich in rust

The Brass Name Plate (2011)
(Bog Cotton)

Winding through reeds

to the crumbling dyke

and the endless sea beyond

Mortality traced out in small blue squares — those four fat years of immortal flat-lining. But this clinical statistic has suddenly taken an alarmingly steep upward curve towards the inscription at the top of the sheet: *Sic Transit.* Now I must play my last card against my deadly adversary Adenocarcinoma (otherwise known as Big C).

At the window

how frantically it beats

against its own reflection

The card is Dr Pfeifer's Magick Protocol. This means it's Harley Street at £300 a throw (just for starters).

So many highly polished brass name plates on every stately door. In the empty waiting room a chandelier hangs above an onyx table. No dog-eared back numbers of *The National Geographic* here, let alone *Hello!* magazine. Instead, bound volumes of surgical journals line the walls. I dip into one and, at the first diagram, hastily replace it. Brisk and bangled, the receptionist ushers me in with a refined gesture.

Between Him

and me

three feet of polished walnut

He drones the litany of pills and potions which constitute the Protocol, and with which I am to stock my medicine cabinet. Zeolite, to rid me of my heavy metals, "taken from volcanic rock and tribo-mechanically activated". Resveratrol, "red wine extract (with grape skins)" and costing more than a good Beaujolais. Then there are more homely pills, like Natto, made from "fermented soya beans", with a reassuring Pomegranate Complex at the bottom of the list. At least nothing here to rack me with the side-effects promised by conventional treatments.

Mesmerised, I gaze out of the window. Behind rows of chimney stacks mares' tails drift in a pale blue sky.

"Mr Jones! Do you have any questions?"

Only the unanswerable ones.

Off-shore wind

the heaving shingle

tumbling my thoughts

[Harley Street — In London, a by-word for the high end of medical treatments.]

Bog Cotton (2011)
(*Bog Cotton*)

Why did he return

to that empty island?

bog-cotton in the wind

— Kenneth White

A warning buoy

rolling heavy in the sound

the tolling of its bell

"Good—I see you've left your baggage behind!" exclaims the sullen ferryman, "for you would have no use for it here." But he is wrong. His passenger has brought a haiku light as a bog cotton flower. Neither speaks of the return passage.

The engine cuts

to a long glide

and the keel grinds in the sand

Just as he remembers it from his youth, it lies beyond the dunes, in the heart of the little island. There the rusty bog enjoys its brief flowering.

Beside a sky-blue pool

shocked

by their wordless whiteness

Silhouetted on the crag above are the ruins of a hermitage. It is like so many on these Isles of the Blessed, set in the Western Sea. Little remains except for a single window, blank to the sky.

"A perfect arch!"

each rough stone

supports the next

He falls to his knees. "Tell me the answer, blustering wind and screaming gulls, quivering bog cotton and rough old stones!" Yet again the wind, the gulls, the bog cotton and the stones all throw back the words in his face.

But finally, as the daylight fades, his question is blown away in the wind, lost in the screams of the gulls, and sinks in the silence of stones. And in his eyes a single warm tear wells up. And the bog cotton? Ah, the dancing bog cotton!

[With grateful acknowledgement to Kenneth White, whose haiku was published in *Handbook for the Diamond Country: Selected Shorter Poems*, 1960-90. Mainstream Publishing, Edinburgh, 1990.]

The Ice Axe (2014)
(after *Bog Cotton*)

No future, past nor present

only a china cup

the tea growing cold

From a sprawling home in a deep valley we are moving to a little house on a sea cliff. The cancer that has been sleeping in my body for years grows suddenly voracious as it moves with us into my bones. The perfect sense of timing of the crab.

Time finally to discard the evidence of my successive selves —
those dear dead enthusiasms and beliefs.

Casting off this long life

the book shelves

not quite stripped bare

And riffling through my fading recollections half the people's
names that should be there are missing.

Faded Brownie snaps

a fleeting smile

gone forever

The rubber band breaks on a dusty bundle of cassettes. Into
the skip with them, vain certainties of a younger voice!

Flecked with swallow shit

Glyndwr's battle flag

hangs limply from the rafters

My seventy-nine year old neighbour comes to collect from the
barn all our well-worn tools no longer useful.

Tangled in rusty chicken wire

my ice axe

the blade still keen

["Brownie snaps" — The Brownie Box Camera, a favourite
early in the last century.

"Glyndwr's battle flag" — Prince Owain Glyndwr, the
romantic hero of Welsh history.]

Ready to Cast Off (2014)
(after *Bog Cotton*)

One key in the lock

in an unseen draught

the other dangles on a ring

Fifty years ago I fled to this little seaside town, the better to live my life. Now I return, the better to die, of a cancer whose time has come. I bring my intervening life packed into some two hundred and fifty haibun in four bulging files, to this tall white house on the edge of a cliff.

All sea and sky

and strutting jackdaws

on a sliver of grass

Every morning, the screaming gulls, the moaning wind and the weary waves breaking on the shore below. Once an avid young man pacing the promenade; now an ancient pondering the shoreline.

There was here an iron ladder I used to climb, now rusted away. But still at nightfall a light comes on at the end of the stone pier. It flashes a warning twice a minute, but how long each minute seems.

Pale above the sea

a waning moon

a waning life

For a novice like me seeing death close up for the first time is as novel as it is scary. My future has gone and my past a distant country. But on a good day, freed fore and aft, a lightness of being.

My Death

my unfamiliar

feral beast

A Change of Address (2014)
(after *Bog Cotton*)

My end game is best played out atop a sea cliff. So we have
exchanged our wrap-around wooded valley for a precarious
perch of sea and sky.

Stretched tight and gleaming

from cape to cape

the sea horizon

Chainsaw and strimmer, dear old friends, sold off. The
wildwood exchanged for a coy lawn. A dinky electric mower
for this, my second childhood. "A better place to die", she
says, turning her face away. And so, day by day, arm in arm,
we promenade our love, as wave follows wave.

A red fishing boat

cutting its white wake

through our winter morning

And now there's chemotherapy, as our penultimate forlorn
hope.

In my mirror

this beardless stranger

deceptively smooth

Biculatimide, degaralex, casodex — those ugly, heartless words of hope that trip off the tongues of oncologists. Mine sketches time lines on the back of some scrap paper. Her Celtic silver wedding ring is just like mine. "Mean survival rate, two years more or less." was her estimate. An attractive woman, in her own way.

Heeling in our fuschias

how I envy their survival rate

My once well-regulated self, cast out into the bleak wastelands of sickness and death. I struggle to find a foothold on the shifting sands of meaning and purpose. My fading routines of must and should. Is this really how Inconceivable Liberation feels!

Each in our so-called easy chair, we enjoy the magnificent sunsets.

Some day

I'll await a sunset such as this

and share its graceful exit.

Another Stay of Execution (2015)
(after *Bog Cotton*)

Another Monday

this life

ruled feint

My oncologist and I are fighting a cool rearguard action against the relentless advance of the Crab. However, she tells me on Tuesday that 2015 might well be a year of grace. By order of the goddess Enzolutomide, conjured up by big pharma at my eleventh hour.

A passing shoal of sunlight on a grey sea

So it's worth phoning my chiropodist for a more serviceable pair of feet, my dentist to extend the longevity of my false teeth, my wine merchant for another crate of Zinfandel, and my editor to postpone the memorial volume yet again.

Surprised by joy

in happy vacancy

I wash the car

How do you expect me to take life seriously, I ask the gods (or kismet or whatever)? This life, unrolled by calendars and clocks, while sun and moon pull the tides in and out, beating upon the promenade outside my window.

Idling in my easy chair

the elusive stuff

that time is made of

*****